CLASSIC MATERIAL
THE HIP-HOP ALBUM GUIDE

D0557894

CLASSIC MATERIAL
THE HIP-HOP ALBUM GUIDE

edited by Oliver Wang

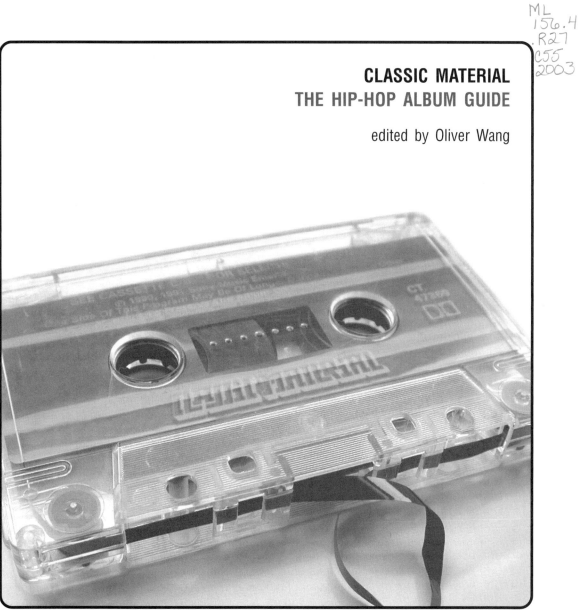

Dedicated to the memory of Jason Mizell (Jam Master Jay):
Goddamn, that DJ made our day.

Copyright © ECW PRESS, 2003

Published by ECW PRESS
2120 Queen Street East, Suite 200, Toronto, Ontario,
Canada M4E 1E2

NATIONAL LIBRARY OF CANADA CATALOGUING
IN PUBLICATION DATA

Classic material: the hip-hop album guide /
Oliver Wang, ed.; foreword by Dante Ross.
ISBN 1-55022-561-8
1. Rap (Music)—Discography.
2. Rap (Music)—History and criticism.
3. Sound recordings—Reviews.
I. Wang, Oliver II. Title
ML156.4.P6H667 2003   016.78242164'90266
C2002-905429-X

Acquisition editor: Emma McKay
Copy editor: Jodi Lewchuck
Interior design and typesetting:
Guylaine Régimbald—Solo Design
Production: Emma McKay
Printing: Transcontinental
Cover design: SekondhandProjects.com
Front cover photo: Paul 107

This book is set in Helvetica and Utopia

The publication of *Classic Material: The Hip-Hop
Album Guide* has been generously supported by
the Canada Council, by the Government of Ontario
through the Ontario Media Development
Corporation's Ontario Book Initiative, by the
Ontario Arts Council, and by the Government of
Canada through the Book Publishing Industry
Development Program. **Canadä**

The opinions expressed in this book are not necessarily those of the publisher.

DISTRIBUTION
Canada: Jaguar Book Group, 100 Armstrong
Avenue, Georgetown, Ontario L7G 5S4

United States: Independent Publishers Group,
814 North Franklin Street, Chicago, Illinois 60610

Europe: Turnaround Publisher Services,
Unit 3, Olympia Trading Estate,
Coburg Road, Wood Green, London N2Z 6T2

Australia and New Zealand: Wakefield Press,
1 The Parade West (Box 2266),
Kent Town, South Australia 5069

PRINTED AND BOUND IN CANADA

ECW PRESS
ecwpress.com

"Every playing of a record is a liberation of a shut-in meaning—a movement, across the groove's boundary, from silence into sound, from code into clarity. A record carries a secret message, but no one can plan the nature of that secret, and no one can silence the secret once it has been sung."

—Wayne Koestenbaum, *The Queen's Throat*

It is a backwater remedy,
bitter and tender memory,
a class E felony,
facing the death penalty.
Stimulant and sedative,
original repetitive,
violently competitive,
a school unaccredited.
—Mos Def, "Hip Hop"

Contents

Acknowledgments

This one goes out to some of my favorites … some of my favorites …

This book wouldn't even exist without the foresight and assistance of ECW's Emma McKay, who initially approached me with the idea of working on a hip-hop–related book. Through the entire process she provided constant support and resources and made its creation possible.

The greatest pleasure I had in putting the book together was the opportunity to work with valued peers and mentors whose work has always been a compelling force in my own life and profession. First, thanks need to go to all the writers who took valuable time out to contribute to this book: Lefty Banks, Reggie Dennis, Allen Gordon, Ernest Hardy, Todd Inoue, Billy Jam, Brett Johnson, Serena Kim, Kris Ex, Melissa Maerz, Jeff Mao, Mosi Reeves, Chris Ryan, Joe Schloss, Zenobia Simmons, and David Toop. This book only works because of your input and insight, and it was a constant inspiration to read your labors of love.

Also, I'd like to acknowledge those who had been willing to write for us but ultimately weren't able to contribute to the book: Sasha Frere-Jones, Charles Aaron, Danyel Smith, Brian Cross (B+), Davey D, Josh DuLac, Havelock Nelson, James Tai, Harry Allen, James Bernard, Tracii MacGregor, and Steven Hager. I'd especially like to acknowledge Josh Kun, whose influence as a writer and mentor is in the book even if his byline isn't.

Of course, all the senior contributing writers, especially Elizabeth Mendez Berry, Peter Shapiro, and Tony Green, get a huge thank you for their participation, input, and support—it goes without saying that I couldn't have done this without you. I'd like to especially thank Jon Caramanica, Hua Hsu, Joseph Patel, and Dave Tompkins for serving as honest and critical sounding boards—not to mention valued friends—over the years. Most of all, I'd like to thank Jeff Chang, who not only invaluably contributed to this book's coming together, but more importantly has been a mentor and role model of incalculable measure. Your friendship, guidance, and motivation are a constant blessing.

On that note, I'm ever thankful for the support of friends and editors who've always encouraged my pursuit of writing, including but not limited to: Jessica Wang, Colleen Chien, Shiree Teng, Ruben Villalobos, Mimi Ho, Ernest Mark, David Leonard, Ed Wong, Sharon Mizota, Robin Li, Liz Lee, Jim Cho, Ed Lee, Mike Pizzo, Chris Veltri, Eothen Alapatt, Jessica Miller, Brian Coleman, Rani Neutill, Jeff Haynes, Melissa Chua, Jessica Miller, Jocelyne Guilbaut, Deborah Wong, Michael Omi, Robin Kelley, B. Ruby Rich, Melissa Maerz, Tom Thompkins, John Payne, T-Love, James Tai, Daniel Chamberlin, Kathryn McGuire, Dan Frosch, Jermaine Hall, and especially Carolyn Lee, Ikuko Sato, and Catherine Huang, who grounded me in ways that made my writing possible in the first place.

Props to all the great hip-hop publications and forums, past and present, for giving us the space to muse, debate, and simply think out loud. Respect is due not only to the national magazines like *ego trip*, *The Source*, *XXL*, *Vibe*, *Rap Pages*, *URB*, etc., but especially to the smaller ones that have often flown under the radar yet have been no less influential in their own way, like *Flavor* and *Bomb Hip-Hop*. Credit is also due to alternative weeklies like the *San Francisco Bay Guardian*, *LA Weekly*, *Minneapolis City Pages*, and *Village Voice* for being some of the last bastions of quality music criticism in a time of glossy-fueled excess. Triple extra-large propers go to Havelock Nelson and Michael Gonzales for their uniformly excellent *Bring the Noise*, and to Gabriel Alvarez, Elliott Wilson, Chairman Mao, Sacha Jenkins, and Brent Rollins, the team behind *ego trip's Book of Rap Lists*—one of the greatest love letters ever written to hip-hop.

This book obviously wouldn't be possible without the music that inspires it. *Classic Material* nods to every single artist who's helped to make hip-hop the most vibrant musical force in the last twenty years—the sonic soundtrack that's accompanied the life passage of entire generations from birth to adulthood. Clearly, the scope of the book can't credit all the countless MCs, DJs, producers, and yes, even A&Rs (what up Dante!) who've helped bring hip-hop to where it is today, but I speak for all the contributors involved when I say that we've never stopped listening.

This book is also for all the writers and critics out there—official and unofficial —who've ever been inspired to argue over the merits of a song, artist, or album simply because hip-hop got into their system and forced its way out through their voices and writing. All of the writers contained herein owe thanks to those who've struggled to give hip-hop an intelligent voice amidst the static. That list is far too massive to include here, but suffice it to say that your contributions have not been forgotten. To all these writers past, present, but especially future …

Right on, write on.

Oliver Wang
Oakland, CA
February 2003

Foreword

I used to try to be the first cat up on some new ish; that way, it really felt like I was the only one holding that gem. The first record I ever had early was the Beastie Boys' *Licensed to Ill*, and I think they were using me as a litmus test. Needless to say, I rocked it on the daily until my ex begged me to give it a break (of course I didn't). I can remember another truly memorable time when Q-Tip played me *The Low End Theory* before it was out and my jaw just hit the floor—I knew I had just heard something revolutionary. Same when I first heard Cypress Hill—I knew I had just heard the future and I made sure my ass knew every lyric six months before the album came out, just 'cause.

Listening to *Mecca and the Soul Broth*er every inch of the way when Pete Rock was making it was a strange one for me, 'cause I knew it was awesome but wasn't sure if the rest of the universe was ready for it. I thought it might be too cerebral but happily, I was wrong. I've only once had the pleasure of working on an album where I knew, in the midst of making it, it would be "that" kind of record. It was Brand Nubian's *One for All*, and we just had too much fun for it not to have been a great one.

When I was first asked to write this foreword for a book by a gang of rap music critics, I gotta say that I was more than a little intimidated. Geez, I was straight shook, but it did make me think: What makes a rap record great? What the heck are the intangibles that make a rap record "the one"? Is it the memories evoked with each listen? Is it the place you're taken to, whether consciously or unconsciously? Or is it that you feel like you know the artist intimately: where they were, what they were doing, what they were going through, and why they made your favorite jam on Side 2 of your crusty old cassette tape from '93?

Could it be that in your dream of dreams, as you recite every lyric to every song for the umpteenth time, a great rap record makes you feel as if you really are the MC spitting that fire, rocking that ill beat? Could it be that when you hear a great rap record, you can't help but jump up and move your ass, get up off your groove thang, and shake what your mama gave you a little harder? (I know a rap record must always inspire the shorties around the way to cold get busy.) Could it be the simple fact that when you have one of those days, a great rap record makes you feel a little better, like you wanna go and kiss your girl or guy, or hug your baby just a little bit harder? Could it be that the record makes you look at the world, raises your awareness, expands your horizons, or paints a picture in your mind? Could it be that the record brings back the days of backspins and windmills, Shelltoes and Pumas, or like the R said, writing your name in graffiti on the wall?

I never thought a rap record mattered for the number of biters it inspired or for the fashion statements it made, but I could be wrong on the latter (I had a N.W.A.-style Carhartt and Dickies outfit, locs and all—but that's another story). Sometimes a rap record's great because of the millions of kids in the burbs it touches; it doesn't have to be ghetto, but it helps. That record might be as close as those kids ever get to the hood, yet in some way it connects these whippersnappers to a message and lifestyle that often is as alien to middle-class white Americans as life on Mars (did we find them green guys yet?).

Could it be that a great rap record stands out simply because there just ain't as many good records in today's cesspool of music?

A great rap record—or a great record, period—changes the sound template forever. It hits you simultaneously in the mind, heart, and booty, and makes your innards rumble in a special way. Rap music is the soundtrack for our lifestyle, the groove in which we live our lives, the theme song to our own private *Starsky and Hutch* show.

The records picked for this book will hopefully show you all what I am rambling on about ...

Dante Ross
New York, NY
August 2002

Introduction

"When I first heard Criminal Minded *I was ... damn, where was I? ... seventh grade battling this other MC ... drinking this 40 in the Lower East Side ..."*

On the intro to their album *Stakes is High,* De La Soul stitch together a patchwork of voices in a communal story of where, when, and how Boogie Down Productions' *Criminal Minded* entered the popular consciousness. What's brilliant about this mnemonic montage is how the stories are both uniquely special *and* universally common. As listeners we each have our own private memories of when music touches us, but we also connect with one another through them. In sharing what we think about KRS-One's commanding baritone or Scott La Rock's boom bap beats, we join each other in a shared place, an audio community we can plug into, if only for a moment. Albums that can transport us away, en masse, cease to be just objects and become experiences.

My first time experiencing an album came when I first heard De La Soul's *3 Feet High and Rising.* It was the summer of 1989, between my junior and senior years of high school, and I took the album with me on a plane trip from Los Angeles up to Santa Cruz. I had run through other hip-hop albums before—Run-D.M.C.'s *Raising Hell,* the Beastie Boys' *Licensed to Ill,* etc.—but De La was something altogether different and far more enthralling. I bugged off the kinetic energy of "Three Is the Magic Number," the sly sexual humor of "Jenifa Taught Me," the bizarre Francophile "Transmitting Live from Mars." But when the opening guitar strains of "Eye Know" came in, my entire world suddenly swirled into the song. I was captivated by its irony-free romantic sentiments and how the sublime beat fed off the pop cheer of Steely Dan's "Peg." I was so jazzed by it that I couldn't wait to share it with my friends sitting next to me on the plane, just so they could feel even a fraction of what I felt. More than just listen to the album, I wanted them to live through the same experience I had just gone through. This was the first time I understood how an album could change your entire worldview.

From "Rapper's Delight" to "It's Like That," "Rebel Without a Pause," "Check the Rhime," "Juicy," "Hard Knock Life," etc., the single has rightfully been the driving force behind hip-hop's popularity for over twenty years now. Yet, while singles may mark the moment, it's been up to the album to lay down a history of hip-hop's passage. Albums were the sign of the music's coming of age, the symbolic transition from its adolescence spent partying and bullshitting to its adulthood focused on taking itself seriously and striving to leave a legacy. With all praises due to the old school where pioneers like Grandmaster Flash, Busy Bee, and the Cold Crush Brothers molded hip-hop through their hit singles, it was albums by the likes of Run-D.M.C., Eric B & Rakim, Public Enemy, and N.W.A. that came to dominate what people knew about hip-hop. In a very real sense, these albums have helped to define hip-hop itself as each new innovation in songwriting or musicmaking expanded our imagination of what hip-hop could be.

As Dante Ross's Foreword suggests, there's no easy formula for determining what makes an album great or memorable. That unpredictability is one of pop music's saving graces amidst the cynicism created by a music industry in which cash rules everything around us. Record labels might try to buy their way into history, but more times than not it's the unknown upstart that finds himself or herself enshrined: KRS-One with *Criminal Minded*, LL Cool J with *Radio*, De La Soul with *3 Feet High and Rising*, Freestyle Fellowship with *To Whom It May Concern*, Nas with *Illmatic*, etc. Ultimately, what elevates these albums over the dozens of failures that litter hip-hop's dustbin is their power to invoke an experience so powerful, it resonates across time and space. The beats become our auditory reality. The lyrics become part of our everyday lexicon. Their release dates mark the calendars of our audio-biographies. These albums are the inspiration behind *Classic Material*—the records that not only are milestones in hip-hop's mercurial evolution, but more importantly, have revolutionized our own understanding of music and, in some ways, the world.

Classic Material focuses on those albums that are most vital to understanding the power, scope, and legacy of hip-hop on its own merits. As such, it's not simply a compiled list of the "best" albums. It makes no attempt to rank the entries in order to proclaim one LP the best ever—if hip-hop could be defined by just a single album, it wouldn't be the complex and enriching music it is today.

Instead, this book attempts to fill a void left curiously vacant: the need for an intelligent, critical guide to hip-hop's most important albums. Havelock Nelson and Michael Gonzales were the first to truly tackle the task in any comprehensive way. Their tome, 1991's *Bring the Noise*, serves both as a reference and an inspiration for *Classic Material*. Since then, only Peter Shapiro's exhaustive *The Rough Guide to Hip-hop* (2001) stands out as a comparable effort. In a book market where you can buy album guides for almost every major genre imaginable, the absence of guides dedicated to hip-hop is glaring and surprising.

This book offers some fifty-odd essays on eighty-plus albums that every rap fan —beginners and veterans alike—should take into consideration. Therefore, it's more selective than the books that have come before it; it's streamlined to stress the importance of the albums themselves rather than rehash already well-documented biographical info. As a result, deciding which albums to include and which to leave out comprised one of the most difficult challenges. It'd be tempting to say that the senior contributors and I made the album selections with all the scientific rigor of paper surveys and focus group studies. But in truth, like most conversations about hip-hop, discussions often took place in informal settings: on all-hour phone calls, in random emails, over evening burrito binges, by shouting at each other in clubs.

In the end we were left with a huge master list and had to whittle it down. Often times, opinions were split on certain albums and deciding what to cut was never an easy decision. But knowing that all of us have our particular listening biases, we wanted to balance everyone's input as much as possible and come up with a final list that was comprehensive in its diversity but not saddled with token choices. For example, while New York albums dominate in many places, careful attention is also paid to the South and West for their important contributions, including some albums that may have flown under people's radar the first time through. Likewise, we didn't want the book to just valorize the present and while we tried to avoid including compilations as much as possible, they were the best way to introduce the sounds of old school pioneers like Grandmaster Flash, Spoonie Gee, and Afrika Bambaataa. Female artists are conspicuously in short supply in the book as well, and while no one would deny that artists like Lil' Kim, Foxy Brown, Yo Yo, Roxanne Shanté, and others have made essential contributions to diversifying hip-hop's perspectives, their albums—many of which have been written and produced by men —have rarely been as influential.

This endeavor, by nature, is canon-building, and part of the irony here is that so much of hip-hop's history has involved crushing canons. Yet, it's also important to at least designate a starting point. *Classic Material* is not arguing that every album *not* included in the pages herein is somehow deficient or unimportant. There's a string of so-called "classic" albums that you'll notice are absent from these pages: *Youngest in Charge, Act a Fool, Whut? Thee Album, Enta Da Stage, Dr. Octogynecologist*, etc. You'd be remiss to simply stop where the book does, but we wanted to create some place for the conversation to begin, and threads of that dialogue begin in the following pages.

On that note, *Classic Material* serves a second, if less transparent, function: To offer up a collection of hip-hop criticism by some of the better writers in the field. This is by no means an attempt to create a volume as ambitious as the *De Capo Book of Rock & Roll Writing*, nor even to follow up on Adam Sexton's curiously ignored 1995 *Rap on Rap*, which collected articles and essays on hip-hop by over forty authors. In his own Introduction Sexton asks, "Why isn't hip-hop criticism better?" noting that its practitioners tended to be split between anti-hip-hop militants and criticism-shy cheerleaders. Even now, approaching a decade later, hip-hop still attracts its share of rabid haters and overly passionate defenders, with a struggling community of writers fighting for a critical space in between.

Part of the problem has been that compared with the modern school of rock criticism that began in the mid 1960s with *Crawdaddy, Creem,* and *Rolling Stone,* hip-hop criticism is still relatively nascent. Although pioneering critics like *Billboard/Village Voice*'s Nelson George and the *New York Daily News*'s Steven Hager were penning groundbreaking essays on hip-hop in the early '80s, the music's oldest (major) magazine, *The Source,* is barely fifteen years old. Other mags like *XXL* and (the now defunct) *ego trip* are younger still. In many ways, the most critical voices throughout much of hip-hop's history haven't been journalists or music writers but the artists themselves—whether Dimples D's taking a swat at the "Sucker DJs" or Common Sense's musing on why "I Used to Love H.E.R."

Hip-hop criticism steadily changed over the course of the '90s with a new generation of writers charting a course that took hip-hop on its own merits rather than as the "new" rock 'n roll or latest musical fad to jock. These writers have built their craft in many places—magazines, of course, but also smaller regional publications, Internet sites, 'zines, and alternative weeklies. From this cadre, *Classic Material* invited over twenty of the strongest scribes to write about the albums that they feel have contributed to hip-hop's explosive growth and depth.

Obviously, we didn't include every worthy critic we could have (next book y'all!), but *Classic Material* tries to gather a team of writers from across geographic, age, experience, ethnic, gender, and—most importantly—taste lines. Given this panoply of talent, there was no style guide to follow, no template to mimeograph. Each of these essays represents a unique voice and perspective, whether it's Jeff Chang taking a sociohistorical look at *Wildstyle,* Elizabeth Mendez Berry tackling the Jay-Z mystique, Ernest Hardy probing Pharcyde's masculinity issues, or Billy Jam dissecting Too $hort's signature "beeeyatch!"

It's not that we expect anyone to go out tomorrow and buy every single one of these albums (though, hey, more power to you if you do). But for any listener serious about hip-hop, who is looking for a primer on its myriad shapes, flows, and forms, *Classic Material* humbly offers itself as a place to begin. Ultimately, *Classic Material* provides only a suggested listening list, and no one is claiming that its interpretation of the reviewed albums is gospel. One of the greatest blessings bestowed upon us is that no one can truly define our musical experiences for us—those are always uniquely our own. So listen forth and be fruitful.

Oliver Wang

Afrika Bambaataa:

by David Toop

Looking for the Perfect Beat 1980–1985 (Tommy Boy, 2001)

Afrika Bambaataa:
Looking for the
Perfect Beat
1980–1985

Afrika Bambaataa's significance in the origination and evolution of hip-hop lies with his title, "Master of Records." Whereas Kool Herc developed the idea of cutting and repeating break sections of funk records and Grandmaster Flash innovated turntable wizardry, Bambaataa's skill lay in programming DJ sets from a huge collection of eclectic records. Neither a musician nor a DJ, his contribution in the studio rested on his role as the ideas man. A dependency on the technical skills of others to translate his utopian visions meant that his solo albums were patchy. The best way to understand his pivotal contribution to hip-hop is to listen to Steve Knutson's compilation of Bam's most important records, *Looking for the Perfect Beat.*

Although his most successful tracks were released by Tommy Boy, Bambaataa first recorded for Paul Winley's Harlem-based label. The two versions of "Zulu Nation Throwdown," both released in 1980, already show a progression of sorts. The Cosmic Force version is typically innocent for its time—catchy chorus, funky beats, disco guitar, and an endless roll call for the MCs—while the Soul Sonic Force follow-up features the tougher rapping of Pow Wow, MC G.L.O.B.E., and Mr. Biggs over an electric piano groove.

Things got more serious with Bambaataa's first release for Tommy Boy. "Jazzy Sensation," a version of Gwen McRae's "Funky Sensation" produced by Arthur Baker and mixed by Shep Pettibone, sold thirty-five thousand copies in New York, clearing Tommy Boy's debts and leading to one of the most significant sessions in hip-hop history. "Planet Rock," released in 1982, gave Bambaataa his first opportunity to merge the diverse music of his DJ sets into one track. Musician John Robie programmed the latest electronic technology and the resulting mix of futuristic keyboards, drum machine beats, and melody lines borrowed from Kraftwerk and Ennio Morricone launched a flood of electro tracks that owed as much to Gary Numan and YMO as they did to Funkadelic.

Hoping to emulate the sales and acclaim accrued by "Planet Rock," Arthur Baker spent eight months recording and mixing "Looking for the Perfect Beat." As with "Planet Rock" and the second version of "Zulu Nation Throwdown," Pow Wow, G.L.O.B.E., and Mr. Biggs supplied the innovative rhymes while the booming, hyper-electronic sound of the record was a perfect simulation of a night at The Funhouse, the Manhattan club where Jellybean played mixes that sounded like arcade games with beats.

"Renegades of Funk" threw everything into the multitrack: Zulu chants, percussion breakdowns, soca, Kraftwerk. In a similar vein, "Frantic Situation" was recorded for *Beat Street*, one of the first films to draw on hip-hop for its story line. "Unity Part 1," a duet with James Brown, was the best of Bambaataa's many collaborations with singers, bands, and producers he admired. Though little more than heavyweight beats programmed by Keith LeBlanc, nods to various JB horn charts, and a series of shouted slogans demanding everything from world peace to crime-free, drug-free fun, it's still an infectious tribute to the Godfather of Soul, who is number one in Bam's pantheon of musical heroes.

Hip-hop's original house band—Keith LeBlanc, Doug Wimbish, and Skip McDonald—shape the heavier, rock-influenced sound of the three cuts that conclude Knutson's compilation. "Who Do You Think You're Funkin' With" and "What Time Is It?" both feature Melle Mel as lead rapper, while "Funk You!" reworks Queen's "We Will Rock You," throwing in song titles from MC5's "Kick Out the Jams" to The Temptations' "Psychedelic Shack."

Listen to this collection in the wrong spirit and you might be tempted to dismiss Bambaataa for self-indulgence and indifferent vocals, but nobody can deny that his inclusive, idealistic, and futuristic vision gave hip-hop its early ambition.

Beastie Boys:

Licensed to Ill (Def Jam, 1986)
Paul's Boutique (Capitol, 1989)
Check Your Head (Grand Royal/Capitol, 1992)

by Joe Schloss

Beastie Boys:
Licensed to Ill

Beastie Boys:
Paul's Boutique

Beastie Boys:
Check Your Head

When I went to the Huge Corporate Music Gigantistore to get the CD *Licensed to Ill*, I found no Beastie Boys music at all. After spinning around like Thelonious Monk for several minutes, I finally realized that the HCMG did in fact have Beastie Boys records—they just didn't put them in the hip-hop section. *They didn't put them in the hip-hop section.* And that—for better or worse—says everything about the Beastie Boys and the way they're treated by people who don't understand them, which seems to be pretty much everybody.

What are you supposed to do about a twisted genetic hybrid with three heads, two turntables, a skateboard, and six hands made entirely of middle fingers that scorns categories, advocates social justice, and tells anyone that can't take a joke to fuck off? The Beasties disrespect authority but respect Biz Markie. They play their own instruments. They were Buddhists before Buddhism was cool. They're a Jewish-feminist version of *Beavis and Butthead*. They're punk rockers, mic rockers, and cultural touchstones. In other words, they steal from everyone and everything and everywhere and smush it all up into something that makes no sense. But since when is that not hip-hop?

The best-known incarnation of the Beastie Boys coalesced as a punk band in 1983, when Ad-Rock (Adam Horovitz) stepped into the preexisting dialectic of MCA (Adam Yauch) and Mike D (Michael Diamond). It wasn't long before they were swept up by the culture and music of hip-hop, becoming first an annoying footnote and eventually an important creative force in lyrics, political activism, sampling, and the use of live instrumentation.

Riding the success of the single and video "Fight for Your Right (To Party)," *Licensed to Ill* was the first rap album to hit number one on the Billboard Pop Charts, which is another way of saying it was the first rap album that lots of white people bought. Which is probably why everyone thinks it's much more rock-oriented than it actually is. Sure they used more metal guitar samples than other artists of the era, but when it comes right down to it, this is a hip-hop album. Period. And that includes all the trimmings, from the 808 booms, War samples, and tight snares, to the story rhymes, progressive flows, and old-school emcee interaction (how many people nowadays trade lines rather than verses?). Some of the cuts like "Paul Revere" and "Brass Monkey" can still turn a standing-around-drinking area into a dance floor. Just because most people who bought the album didn't see it for what it was, it doesn't mean that *Licensed to Ill* wasn't about creative, funny, obnoxious, intelligent hip-hop.

Three years later, having dropped Rick Rubin's rockadelia for the dirty grooves of the Dust Brothers, the Beasties released *Paul's Boutique*, a natural companion to Public Enemy's *It Takes a Nation of Millions to Hold Us Back* (1988) and De La Soul's *Three Feet High and Rising* (1989), one of the first fully realized works of sample-based art. Taking snares, horn hits, and guitar stabs from Idris Muhammad, Sly Stone, and folk/blues guitarist David Bromberg, *Paul's Boutique* set the standard for turning a diverse batch of sounds into a cohesive motherfucker. The lyrics, meanwhile, continued on the path set by *Licensed to Ill*, painting portraits of the yahoo's quotidian life in Ed Koch's New York: getting kicked out of the Palladium, watching a guy reading *El Diario* on the subway, learning about the role of fate and chance in human life through offtrack betting. This time, though, the album was infused with a sly sophistication; references to Galileo, Jack Kerouac, and Japanese baseball great Sadaharu Oh suggest that the bad-boy posturing may have been wearing thin, even for the Beastie Boys. Or maybe not—who could tell? Listening to it today, the most striking thing about this album is that it sounds like it came out two or three years later than it actually did; it was a 1991 hip-hop album released in '89.

On 1992's *Check Your Head*, the Beastie Boys stepped out from behind the curtain and started to sound like real people. And while we can all agree that extending the Wizard of Oz metaphor here would be cheap—why, they had heart, brains, and courage all along, but they just didn't know it! —there would be truth in it. *Check Your Head* marks the moment when they began to really trust their instincts and as a result, it is their best work by far. By chopping up the music they loved—without regard to demographics, marketing categories, or boundaries—and playing it back live on real instruments, the Beastie Boys took responsibility for being grown-up white people in hip-hop without boring everyone with long rationalizations about how down they were.

Each snare hit on *Check Your Head* was so saturated in reverb and compression and distortion that the album sounded like it was recorded at the bottom of a well and broadcast on AM radio to a speaker in the back of a Brooklyn bodega. In fact, on songs like "Pass the Mic" and "So What'cha Want," the emcees' voices were so distorted that you could barely understand what they were saying, even if you wanted to. And that was the craziest part: you *wanted* to understand them. With their newfound musical maturity came an unexpected and compelling lyrical openness. OK, so the message wasn't "Stay away from drugs" and "Be a father to your child," but it was "Hey—here's something that's been on my mind" and "When you finish that beer, we should talk." After all the adolescent hijinks and retarded sexuality that had made them popular in the first place, the new approach set the stage for the weird punch line to their strange career: Women *love* them. No, seriously. Self-possessed, grown-up women actually enjoy listening to the Beastie Boys. How many other male hip-hop artists can claim that audience? A Tribe Called Quest, maybe, but whom else?

Although the Beastie Boys' career path is well worn, it's been a while—a long while—since anyone else has had both the vision and the talent to follow it. It is the path of the gimmicky teen pop star that against all odds actually evolves into… an artist. A long time ago, when pop stars had talent and record companies cared, such an evolution wasn't quite so rare. Artists like Stevie Wonder, Marvin Gaye, and the Beatles gained fame as cute media darlings, then suddenly took a sharp left turn into intense personal revelation, political stridency, and weird musical experiments. In their own way, the Beastie Boys sailed directly from drunken bravado to Buddhist compassion with no plan and no excuses. They embraced the Dalai Lama with the same arms that a few years earlier had clutched only beer, strippers, and a giant hydraulic penis. How many other contemporary artists could go from "Fight for Your Right (To Party)" to "Bodhisattva's Vow" in six years? How many would want to? And if America's musical megamarts want to call it "Pop/Rock/Soul" that's all right with me, because it only means hip-hop still has the power to confuse the small-minded. Besides, they're just jealous—it's the Beastie Boys.

Beatnuts: S/T (Relativity, 1994)
Diamond: Stunts, Blunts & Hip Hop (Chemistry/Mercury, 1992)
Main Source: Breaking Atoms (Wild Pitch, 1990)
Pete Rock & CL Smooth: Mecca and the Soul Brother (Elektra, 1992)

by Oliver Wang

Beatnuts:
S/T

Diamond:
Stunts, Blunts & Hip
Hop

Call 'em the chairmen of the board, the aural architects of hip-hop's sonic blueprint in the early 1990s. Whereas the New School era from the mid- to late 1980s saw the proliferation of larger-than-life hip-hop (both in scope and attitude), the early '90s brought the focus inward, leading to a more introspective aesthetic that required a complementary musical shift. The funk-emblazoned sound of pioneering '80s producers like Marley Marl, the Bomb Squad, and Ced Gee captured the aggressiveness of the New School era perfectly, but for this new hip-hop sensibility, new sonic sources had to be mined once James Brown's *Star Time* dimmed and the P-Funk Mothership was pirated.

The new generation of beat barons began to turn to more obscure or unconventional sources for their sampling fix. Improvements to technology helped, as most (save Large Professor) abandoned the venerable but limited E-Mu SP-1200 for the more flexible, higher capacity Akai MPC series samplers that allowed for longer loops and more sophisticated editing. But the shift was primarily in sound and texture; these newer producers looked to the world of jazz, soul, and other rare groove sources for inspiration, creating a more relaxed sonic attitude that aimed for the intimacy of the backroom lounge rather than the spectacle of the rock arena.

Introspective isn't the word that comes to mind with the Beatnuts. The 'Nuts trio—Psycho Les, Juju, and Fashion—are ignorant and they wholeheartedly celebrate this attitude in the chorus from *Intoxicated Demons*'s "Psycho Dwarf": "I want to fuck/drink beer/and smoke some shit." Throughout their history, the

Beatnuts have been hip-hop's sonic equivalent to cotton candy: not exactly the most filling of treats, but it sure as hell tastes good. And while they may have lacked the more reflective qualities of their peers, musically they stood with the best of them.

These three producers-*cum*-MCs have surprisingly slick flows and though they never say anything mind-shattering, they sound good doing it, which makes for wildly fun party tunes and brag-gadocio cuts. There are no clear-cut "best" songs on their debut album; it's all a matter of temperament since almost all of the material is good. For those looking to get down on the heavy funk, the ripping guitars and twitching rattles on "Are You Ready" hit like a roundhouse, while "Rik's Joint" is all soothing jazz chords and mellow vibes. "Get Funky" is pure slickness with its guitar loop and driving drum break, while the puerile "Lick the Pussy" is equally salacious in its syrupy soul sample lifted from Tyrone Davis. The only possible complaint one could make is that the Beatnuts aren't doing all that much to their sources—this is an album almost exclusively built on unchanging loops, save for a few chorus elements added to a handful of songs. It's certainly not as sophisticated as Pete Rock or Large Professor's compositions, though in the end, if it's this much fun to listen to does it really matter?

Diamond D's *Stunts, Blunts & Hip Hop* is remarkably similar to the Beatnuts' album, though Diamond is a decidedly more talented—and less profane—rapper than any of the 'Nuts. Mentored into producing by the likes of Lord Finesse, Jazzy Jay, and his own first group, Ultimate Force, Diamond's mic skills were unexpected—hence the title to his first single, "Best Kept Secret." But more than just punching out boast after boast, Diamond shows some dimensionality with his subject matter; notice the fugitive narratives on "I'm Outta Here" or the playful gender wars on "Red Light, Green Light."

The real gems on the album are his beats. Like the Beatnuts, he mostly finds great loops, though on rare exceptions such as "I Went for Mine" and "Feel the Vibe," Diamond dabbles in more sophisticated layers and arrangements. But as his song "K.I.S.S. (Keep It Simple, Stupid)" suggests, Diamond squeezes out impressive mileage from his crate-rummaging, including stellar production on songs like "Check One, Two," a dramatic mid-tempo construction built on a simple two-bar blues sample and the title track, with its bizarre, otherworldly sound. The album's only real misstep is "Confused," an unconditionally awful crossover attempt at marrying sappy R&B rhythms and lackluster rhymes.

From a connoisseur's point of view, much of Diamond's best producing followed *Stunts* on a variety of one-off projects for everyone from the Fugees to Mos Def to Fat Joe. But back in 1992,

Diamond (along with Pete Rock) set the standard for what a production-driven album could sound like. (Note: The CD contains two excellent songs, "Feel the Vibe" and "I Went for Mine," that are not featured on the vinyl versions of the album.)

If the Beatnuts and Diamond were learned scholars of the diggin' in the crates school, they all studied under one of hip-hop's greatest teachers, the Large Professor. Himself a disciple of unsung producer/engineer legend Paul C., Large Professor joined up with the Canadian DJ duo of Sir Scratch and K-Cut in the late '80s and together, as Main Source, they dropped *Breaking Atoms* in 1990. Looking back, it's easy to see how ahead of its time the album was. Large Professor is far and away the best rapper among his peers with extraordinary songwriting capacity: look only as far as the instant classic on relationship strife, "Looking at the Front Door"; the take on social hypocrisy, "Peace Is Not the Word to Play"; and the brilliant police brutality critique, "Just a Friendly Game of Baseball." As a producer, Large Professor thinks in complete song structure, never focusing on one single element—a loop, a break—but always juggling them inunison. For example, "Snake Eyes," which begins the album, has no less than five different samples running through it, including an Ike Turner piano vamp, a Johnnie Taylor bassline, and a Jesse Anderson flute melody. "Peace Is Not the Word" is the album's musical climax, as Large Professor spits a quick set of verses and then lets his beats do the talking as the rest of the song continues to build and shift strictly as an instrumental. It'd be a tour de force in any era, but Main Source came up with this in 1990 when most other producers were still getting mileage out of James Brown's "Funky Drummer." It's no wonder that even ten-plus years after its initial release, *Breaking Atoms* sounds as fresh, vital, and innovative as ever.

On the other hand, Pete Rock & CL Smooth's *Mecca and the Soul Brother* sounds dated, but only because it so thoroughly defined its era that it's impossible not to associate the album's songs with that precious post–New School and pre-*Chronic* moment in hip-hop history. Though Dr. Dre has unleashed scores of copycats upon pop music, Pete Rock is the one most responsible for the legions of underground beat makers that have followed him, acolytes to his particular aesthetic. Of his brethren, Pete is arguably the most sophisticated, playing with carefully constructed arrangements that show sampling's true musical potential: what happens when someone simply takes the time to play with the various pieces. That's why songs on this album like "They Reminisce Over You" and "Straighten It Out" have become all-time hip-hop classics—they reflect not only Pete's unmatched ears for outstanding samples, but also his ability to craft them into something greater than the sum of their parts. Pete's particular gift has been in his layering, his ability to juggle in any number of different elements—a bassline twiddle here, a keyboard tinkle there, not to mention horns. Pete Rock's signature sound of this era was his horns; he brought them in full blast on tracks like "Can't Front on Me," "Return of the Mecca," and "The Basement."

Main Source:
Breaking Atoms

Of course, Pete was only half of the equation and his MC partner CL Smooth (Mecca to Pete's Soul Brother) plays an integral role in the album's success. Over time, CL's rhymes have become more accessible but on this album, he excels in a stream of consciousness flow of provocative abstraction. It's not that he doesn't make sense, but his poetics are rarely straightforward and never simple, which is best exemplified on cuts like "Return of the Mecca," "Wig Out," and "They Reminisce Over You." CL favors clever plays on words and turns of phrase, whereas Pete Rock kicks down a more basic, freestyle-flavored flow that gets the job done even if it's not as dazzling as his tracks. In a sense, this was the last great hurrah of the New School era before the double whammy of West and East Coast gangsta/thuggery reclaimed hip-hop's imagination. But even after myriad changes in the music's direction since then, *Mecca and the Soul Brother* signaled a pinnacle moment in otherwise mercurial times. (Note: The vinyl version of this album contains a remix of "Mecca and the Soul Brother" not available on the CD.)

**Pete Rock &
CL Smooth:**
Mecca and
the Soul Brother

Big Daddy Kane:
Long Live the Kane (Cold Chillin', 1988)
It's a Big Daddy Thing (Warner Bros., 1989)
Biz Markie: Goin' Off (Cold Chillin', 1988)

by Kris Ex

Big Daddy Kane:
Long Live the Kane

Big Daddy Kane:
It's a Big Daddy Thing

Biz Markie:
Goin' Off

History has by and large written Rakim Allah as *the* microphone god, but it wasn't always thus. Before history was written, the "best emcee" argument invariably pitted Rakim against Juice Crew All-Star Big Daddy Kane. (That heated debate is reincarnated today in the Jay-Z versus Nas argument. It's no small coincidence that Jay-Z briefly hung out in the studio under Kane's tutelage while Nas, the pensive and philosophical wordsmith, worshiped at the altar of Rakim.) And this isn't simple, pompous, navel-gazing music critic bullshit here, either. This was real a competition. Legend has it that Kane, a Juice Crew DJ and ghostwriter who made crew members Roxanne Shanté and Biz Markie's shit tighter, put Ra on notice when he spit what would later become "Raw" a cappella at Ra's own birthday barbecue. ("Here I am / R-A-W / A terrorist, here to bring trouble to / Phony emcees / I move on and seize / I just conquer and stomp another rapper with ease / 'Cause I'm at my apex and others are below / Nothing but a milliliter, I'm a kilo / Second to none, making emcees run / So don't try to step to me, 'cause I ain't the one.") The same legend asserts that Kane later suggested a monetary wager for a stage confrontation, but Ra rightfully refused.

Why? Lyrically, Kane was not to be toyed with. Ra may be the ultimate microphonist in the eyes of many, but he was no battle emcee. What put Kane over the top was his delivery. Where Ra was a quiet storm of measured cool, Kane was a human hurricane of ferocious flow, monstrous metaphor, superb simile, jaunty jest, and pithy punch line ("You're just a butter knife, I'm a machete / That's made by Ginsu / Wait until when you / Try to front, so I can chop into / Your body / Just because you try to be bassin' / *Friday the 13th*, I'ma play Jason"). And *Long Live the Kane* is one of the best, most complete hip-hop records ever made. Ever. Verbwise, there's no shortage of alliteration, vocab, intelligence, or humor. The classic boastfests are there: "Raw," "Ain't No Half-Steppin'," "Just Rhymin' with Biz." Musically, there's just as much depth: Marley Marl's history-making sampling techniques that created soundscapes of inverted and sped-up instrumentation with vocal snippets and precise scratches layered atop deep bass; cascading walls of sound that are full of noise but not noisy; live park-jam exuberance. Kane covered many bases, sandwiching his loverman experimentation ("The Day You're Mine") in between hard jams early on in the record and dropping knowledge on the last track, "Word to the Mother (Land)." Over a decade before Nas would create a Kurtis Blow–inspired ghettopia with "If I Ruled the World (Imagine That)" or Nelly would fashion his peaceful urban renewal on "Nellyville," Kane and Marley sampled the Staple Singers on "I'll Take You There" to muse on a promised land where "You can hang at a jam till the break of dawn / And leave without your Bally shoes getting stepped on."

If Kane's revisionist program was too heavy, there was always Biz Markie's *Goin' Off*. Largely written by Kane and produced entirely by Marley Marl, *Goin' Off* featured the enduring seriousness of "The Vapors," which depicted a syndrome that, amazingly enough, had not been named and has yet to be successfully renamed. The tales of Biz's hard times in the neighborhood and his cousin/

DJ's struggles on the road to fame before being jocked by the former haters are about as deep as it gets. *Goin' Off* was created as a dance album in an era when hip-hop was no longer being looked at as essentially dance music. Relatively sparse and chunky, there's nothing but a good time on "Pickin' Boogers," where Biz recounts his predilection for the title activity; "Albee Square Mall," an ode to downtown Brooklyn's meeting ground; "Nobody Beats the Biz," fashioned after a local TV commercial; and the title track, where Biz drops non sequiturs like "You wanna get dissed? / Then try to get illy with me the inhuman / Because I'm like boomin' / Reagan is the pres, but so was Harry Truman." On "This is Something for the Radio," Marley invents the remix with five minutes of Jamaican dub-influenced funk as a platform for Biz to babble shout-outs and thank-yous like a drunk Academy Award recipient.

Meanwhile, Kane was honing his best rhymes for 1989's *It's a Big Daddy Thing*. The album was not so much a follow-up to *Long Live the Kane* as it was a continuation or a redux. As on his debut, Kane starts off with the title track and shows sublime prowess when talking about his sublime prowess on cuts like "Another Victory," "Wrath of Kane," and "Warm It Up, Kane." He once again goes for midnight love with "To Be Your Man" and makes heartfelt, but not corny, overtures toward Black pride and social uplift on "Children R the Future,"

"Young, Gifted and Black," and "Rap Summary (Lean on Me Remix)." But *Big Daddy Thing* is also a more mature thing. On "Calling Mr. Welfare," Kane takes a look out the project windows to make poignant observations that combine insight, storytelling ability, and humor: "Pimp Daddy's gone and as he maxes and relaxes / She can't even sue for money, pushers don't pay taxes / So what to do? Oh dear / To feed ten mouths, she had to call on Mr. Welfare." Kane takes his loverman status into overdrive, bringing in New Jack Swing architect Teddy Riley for "I Get the Job Done." He also indulges in Blaxploitation fantasy on "Big Daddy's Theme" and gives the same ladies he woos elsewhere the backhand on "Pimpin' Ain't Easy" ("And if you wanna see a smooth black Casanova—bend ovah!").

The music on *It's a Big Daddy Thing* is richer and more developed, if not always more engaging, than on *Long Live the Kane*. There's a better sense of arrangement, timing, spacing, and surprise—it's the sound of a producer and emcee gaining confidence in each other and themselves—culminating in what would become Kane's signature song, "Smooth Operator." With mellow sax grooves, triumphantly cool horns, a bassline from Mary Jane Girls' "All Night Long," and small vocal flourishes slinking around gully boasts ("I give nightmares to those who compete / Freddy Kruger walking on Kane Street"), "Smooth Operator" set down the modus operandi for the Notorious B.I.G.'s bigger radio hits. (Note that Kane's DJ Mister Cee is the same Mister Cee that gave Big's career a start.)

When people talk about classic hip-hop records, these three are criminally unheralded. And when talking about the best emcee, people often overlook Kane; in the case of Biz Markie, he's viewed as a character and a punch line before a musical entertainer. It's undeniable that Kane's later work failed to knock 'em out the box like his original one-two combination; likewise, Biz's legacy is forever marred by the sample clearance issues that surrounded his 1991 *I Need a Haircut*. But *Long Live the Kane* and *It's a Big Daddy Thing* proved beyond a shadow of a doubt that Kane was indeed, as his name stated, King Asiatic Nobody's Equal. He loved to brag, but damn he was good. If mics were guns, he'd be Clint Eastwood. As for the Biz, well, he was just magnificent. But so was the Seven.

Boogie Down Productions:

Criminal Minded (B-Boy, 1987; M.I.L. 1997; rereleased as *The Best of B-Boy Records* [Landspeed, 2001])

By All Means Necessary (Jive/Novus, 1988)

by Jeff Chang

**Boogie Down
Productions:**
Criminal Minded

**Boogie Down
Productions:**
By All Means Necessary

KRS-One has called himself a teacher, a philosopher, a metaphysician, and most controversially, hip-hop itself. Of the four, the easiest to defend is his claim to the last. His lectures can hurdle logic, his philosophy never coheres, his metaphysics sometimes sounds like sci-fi. He's less interesting as a scholar than as a wise guy, less compelling as a philosopher than as a philistine-crusher, less fun as a spiritualist than as a skeptic. We love him not because he thinks very deeply—which he clearly does—but because he has to *shout* that he does. He's always the underdog struggling to earn respect. Even when he's on top, he acts like he's trying to come up. We love him for the same reasons we love hip-hop.

That's why his best albums remain his earliest—back when Lawrence Krisna Parker was just another kid breathing fire and scrambling for a toehold in Reagan's Amerikkka and Koch's New York City. For the post–civil rights generation, his story is archetypal. Homeless, hungry, and hustling and possessed of mother wit, insatiable curiosity, and boundless spirit, he ended up in a Bronx shelter where he impressed his social worker, Scott Sterling. Known by night as DJ Scott La Rock, Sterling gained Parker's undying respect by taking him to his first hip-hop club gig. Shortly after, they hooked up with producer Ced Gee to cut "South Bronx" and "The Bridge Is Over," monumental records that toppled the Queensbridge-based Juice Crew and forever sealed the Bronx's place and their own names in the history of hip-hop.

After Run-D.M.C. crossed over to massive success, hip-hop's next generation was more interested in returning to the hood, mainly writing for the average New Yorker. Their music was slower and denser. Rhymes were recited with less arena bravado and more casual menace. The scale of *Criminal Minded* was intimate; it was made for the headphones and KRS-One delivered his lines as if he was standing right next to you wearing a knowing, confident smirk.

His words were weapons; he described himself as the arrow, Scott as the crossbow. The effect was unsettling, almost lurid—it dared you to blink. For fans in the boroughs, there was the headrush of self-recognition. For critics, KRS's intellect leavened the coarseness. For hip-hoppers outside of New York—who were also hearing Schoolly D, Toddy Tee, and Ice-T in the summer of '86—the record was part of the crest of change. Run-D.M.C. sounded like throwbacks, rapping that they were "proud to be black." To BDP, that fact was, to use one of KRS-One's favorite phrases, "self-evident."

The album cover, like Public Enemy's *Yo! Bum Rush the Show*, depicted Scott and KRS literally underground in a dim basement a generation after COINTELPRO, readying the return of black militancy to the surface. They were bunkered in the Bronx with handguns, an ammo belt, a grenade, a phone, and a B-Boy Records plaque. The record—with "9mm Bang"'s gleeful bloodletting and "The P Is Free"'s crackpipe sexual politics—was far from an NAACP-approved manifesto. KRS-One said his name stood for "Knowledge Reigns Supreme Over Nearly Everybody," and he meant it.

On the eve of their major label signing in 1987, La Rock was killed while trying to settle a dispute between then crew member D-Nice and others. The tragedy pushed the twenty-two-year-old KRS-One into a starring role. He responded by posing like Malcolm X on the cover of *By All Means Necessary* toting an Uzi in a self-defense stance and cutting a record called "Stop the Violence." He wrote uplift and menace into the same couplet: "We gotta put our heads together and stop the violence / 'Cause real bad boys move in silence." Maybe it was contradictory, but the times called for it: 1987 had begun with massive protests over the Howard Beach incident, a reminder that racist violence was not yet history. Scott's death pointed to the fact that black-on-black violence wasn't either. This was no time for fretting over ideology.

Rakim was rapping about what self-esteem could do for the individual and for the race. KRS-One became the living proof. When he shouted, "I'm still number one!" he signaled that Scott's death, their struggles, and the struggle of Africans in Amerikkka would never be in vain. He announced that he was ready to embody hip-hop's fuck-you contrarianism. Why be all things to all people? Moving things forward required doing for self. "Some people look at me and see negativity /

Some people look at me and see positivity," he rhymed. "But when I see myself, I see creativity."

KRS-One was now the post-white, post-ideological "Wild One," rebelling against whatever counted as the prevailing wisdom, trying to topple whoever claimed to be King. On "Illegal Business," he captured the emerging protest movement's disgust with drug war hypocrisy. On "My Philosophy," a sequel to "Poetry," he proclaimed his arrival by stepping on some Adidas Shelltoe shoes: "I don't 'walk this way' to portray or reinforce stereotypes of today." The next generation is taking over, KRS-One seemed to say, and I'll lead the charge—bring them *all* on.

In retrospect, KRS-One's confrontational rhymes say "Judge me by my enemies." And the list is now a long one: pacifists and warmongers, academics and illiterates, police and thieves, white supremacists and Afrocentrists, Christians and anti-Christians, the Juice crew and most of the old BDP crew. It's clear his career has become an unending war of position. "Whether peace by war, or peace by peace, the reality of peace is scary," he said in 1988. "But we must get there, one way or another, by all means necessary." This perpetual warrior has been all about the "getting there," the fight—a perfect icon for a generation suspicious of all allies and doubtful about ever getting to the mountaintop.

by Serena Kim

Brand Nubian: One for All (Elektra, 1990)

"The devil's still causing trouble among the righteous people/Drugs in our communities (That ain't right)/Can't even get a job (That ain't right)/Poisoning our babies."
—Brand Nubian, "Wake Up"

Brand Nubian:
One for All

In 1990, when *One for All* by Brand Nubian hit the streets, racial tension hurt like a bad hangover from the '80s. Apartheid festered. The Howard Beach incident was still fresh in people's minds, while the Crown Heights and LA riots waited impatiently in the future. Black Muslim thought seemed to make sense. Forget turning the other cheek, it was eye for an eye. If the Nation of Islam was empowering for Malcolm X in the '60s, the pseudotheology espousing black superiority seemed like an antidote for oppression to millions of black youth in the early '90s. Rap groups who claimed Five Percenter allegiance—like Eric B. and Rakim, Poor Righteous Teachers, and X-Clan—were taking hip-hop in an exciting, new, and more political direction. Among the revolutionaries was a talented Bronx-bred rap group called Brand Nubian.

The ideology of the Five Percenters didn't quite hold up under scrutiny, though; it more resembled a cult than the Orthodox Islam of the motherland. As devout Black Muslims, the members of Brand Nubian were wrapped up in hypocrisy. They said they "never ate pork, can't deal with the swine"—as if that alone was enough to claim submission to Allah. They said they respected the fairer sex, but then there was "Slow Down," a caustic criticism of drug-dependent women. "Bitch get a job," spit Puba, "From me you won't rob/'Cause I'll smack you with a hose filled with sand." Granted, he was talking about crackheads. But crackheads are people too.

The album was executive produced by Dante Ross, a white Lower East Side wunderkind who had cut his teeth as a roadie for Eric B. and Rakim. It was Ross who signed Brand Nubian to Elektra (as well as Queen Latifah and De La Soul to Tommy Boy). Along with co-Stimulated Dummy Jon Gamble, Ross remixed the still relevant crate staple "Wake Up." Even though Brand Nubian thought of white people as devils, they trusted Ross enough to helm their project as A&R.

Despite their obvious contradictions, Brand Nubian were masters of their time (and not just because of Puba's pre-Nubian history with the old-school clique Masters of Ceremony). Sadat X, Grand Puba, Lord Jamar, and DJ Alamo collectively crafted righteous street parables that were edifying and gratifying, if not terrifying at times. Besides hatred, Brand Nubian preached hip-hop sermons on enlightenment, equality, and justice. And *One for All* was a dope album that could be played straight through, with no fast-forwards and many savory rewinds. Their debut was conscious, but it wasn't boring like so much of what passes as "conscious hip-hop" nowadays.

Puba was a charismatic lyricist and Sadat X (aka Derek X) flourished under his tutelage. On "All for One," the scholarly emcee spits witty lines like "Read my book, it contains many pieces of verses / I took the time to delete all the curses / So moms reach deep in your purses," sounding so promising and innovative—nothing like his flat solo debut, *The State of New York vs. Derek Murphy.* Puba was still nicer. Back in those days, everyone —even on the West Coast—thought he was the greatest rapper in the world. With his scratchy, nasal voice and springy delivery, Puba dropped science on "Concerto in X Minor": "I wanted to get

violent, but I'm a lover of black mothers / And black mothers need sons / Not children that's been killed by guns." Now give that to your A&R man.

"Concerto"'s funky piano sample from the Cannonball Adderley and Joe Zawanul collabo "Country Preacher" was just one of the many fresh beats on *One for All*. Every tune benefited from the cozy SP-1200 drum machine that reigned supreme at the time. Even on "Dedication," Puba's touching outro to all of his emcee peers and mentors, the kick drum tumbles with the warmth of a good dryer on a cold day. The soulful extrapolation of the Funkadelic guitar lick on "Brand Nubian" makes the postmillennial listener long for a simpler, more analog time. And the oft-overlooked album cut "Who Can Get Busy Like This Man" is a sinuous hip-hop/ reggae combo that stood head and shoulders above all the other hip-hop/reggae songs that were once as mandatory as thug anthems are today.

Well, times sure have changed. Even a peep about black nationalism sounds the death knell for a rap career. Who can blame rappers for keeping their lips sealed about politics? In 1990, when hip-hop hadn't yet been co-opted by the mainstream, it wasn't so bad when Brand Nubian cheered, "We're gonna drop the bomb on the Yacub crew / We're gonna drop the bomb on the caveman crew." But now that bombs have dropped, those lyrics send chills. And like all good poetry, it proved prophetic.

by Lefty Banks

Common Sense: Resurrection (Relativity, 1994)

Common Sense:
Resurrection

Some albums double as memoirs, but Common's entire catalog reads autobiographically. His first LP, 1992's *Can I Borrow a Dollar?*, is a portrait of the artist as a young hoodrat: talented but cocky, smirking his way through lesser MCs when he's not ass-slapping betties for fun. By his third and fourth albums, *One Day It Will All Make Sense* (1996) and *Like Water for Chocolate* (1999), Common is transformed: mature and focused on adult responsibilities, fatherhood, and raising social consciousness. Such an evolution needs a bridge and for Common, the transition from brash b-boy to budding boho is made on the aptly named *Resurrection*.

If *Can I Borrow a Dollar?* captures the Chicago MC in all his high school boldness, *Resurrection* finds Common in the throes of collegiate consciousness, imbued with a newfound righteousness that's jagged around the edges, but unexpectedly introspective and thoughtful. This shift, trading in Cabrini for the coffeehouse, is evident on his seminal hit "I Used to Love H.E.R.," where Common questions and bemoans hip-hop's gimmickry and commercialism by talking about the music through the metaphor of a woman (i.e., "Stressing how hardcore and real she is / She was really the realest, before she got into showbiz"). Instantly, Common became the spokesman for underground heads everywhere who were frustrated with the perceived mainstreaming of hip-hop (and mind you, this was in pre-Puffy 1994). Moreover, Common, as a Chicago MC, avoided bicoastal allegiances and held the begrudging respect of those on the East as a student of their aesthetic while those out West embraced him for being a fellow NYC outsider.

Unlike the uneven performances on the previous album, Common's lyricism is virtuosic on *Resurrection*. There's still a hint of playfulness in his distinctive flow, but he's able to compose far more complex rhyme schemes. Like a verbal pinball, he exerts a kinetic momentum, like when he drops this tongue-twisting line for "Resurrection": "I analyze where I rest my eyes / And chastise the best of guys with punch lines / I'm Nestle when it's Crunch-time." And more than just braggin' and boastin', Common proves exceptionally versatile as well by flipping party jams ("Maintaining"), proffering black capitalist manifestos ("Chapter 13"), saluting Chicago ("Nuthin' to Do"), or simply rhyming his ass off ("Orange Pineapple Juice").

What makes the album complete is the production, mostly handled by No I.D., with a small assist from Ynot. Though No I.D. would later record his own solo album, *Resurrection* remains his best work of note—as impressive a debut effort as you could hope to hear. Clearly influenced by the likes of Pete Rock and A Tribe Called Quest, No I.D.'s jazz- and soul-inspired tracks rank among the best of the era. He does a remarkably good job making tracks out of songs that most would otherwise ignore—small one- and two-bar loops from unassuming (though laudably obscure) sources like jazz/rock fusionist Archie Whitewater or pop instrumentalists Hot Buttered Soul. Equally impressive is how No I.D. matches the mood of the song as demanded by Common's lyrics; on a braggadocio cut like "Watermelon," the rolling rhythm that No I.D. engineers synchs with Common's own verbal torrent. Likewise, the bright perkiness of the pianos on "Maintaining" reflects the celebratory tone of the song perfectly. Arguably, Common's later *Like Water for Chocolate* is the superior artistic album in terms of scope and vision. But while *Resurrection* may be simpler in its pleasures, those pleasures are also more intensely felt. There's a tangible joyfulness that runs through, as if Common is discovering his full gifts and can't wait to show them off. In a real way, that's exactly what *Resurrection* is: a coming of age album for an artist finally blossoming into his full potential.

Company Flow: Funcrusher Plus (Rawkus, 1997)
Cannibal Ox: The Cold Vein (Definitive Jux, 2001)

by Peter Shapiro

Company Flow:
Funcrusher Plus

Cannibal Ox:
The Cold Vein

In hip-hop, like in all popular music, attitude counts for a lot—if not everything. But seemingly unlike all other popular music, hip-hop requires that you have the goods to back it up. It's fine to run around proclaiming your independence and underground status, but when you put out a record that sounds like you're just biding time until Roc-A-Fella's Damon Dash gives you the nod, it just doesn't wash.

During their six-year life span, Company Flow were indeed "independent as fuck." While everyone around them was rushing to associate themselves with the latest luxury brand, Co Flow had the gumption to declare, "Fuck Time-Warner and its affiliates." They relished the freedom that their position in the hip-hop underbelly gave them and developed the most uncompromising aesthetic in contemporary hip-hop. These angry young men and their sinister synth stabs and raw, fuck-you drums created a kind of hip-hop that wouldn't know jiggy if Lil' Kim, wearing nothing but a Fendi bag, came up and shook her thing in its face. While this may sound perilously close to death metal, Co Flow grew up when hip-hop was all about stripped down, brutal, crunching funk, and they have maintained a commitment to that project ever since.

After a series of 12-inches on their own Official Recordings label and a number of electrifying appearances on WKCR's *Stretch Armstrong* show during the mid-'90s, El-P, Mr. Len, and Bigg Jus signed to indie titans Rawkus and released the landmark *Funcrusher Plus* album in 1997. Unlike so many records that herald a paradigm shift, *Funcrusher Plus*'s impact hasn't lessened over time. It's still mean, intimidating, and thoroughly aggressive: the drums will still cave your chest in; El-P will still have you scratching your head. *Funcrusher Plus* is ugly and relentlessly masculine: you can imagine Henry Rollins, Norman Mailer, Robert Anton Wilson, and Philip K. Dick doing bench presses to it. There are grooves buried in here, but they've been compressed in a trash compactor and taken out to a landfill on Staten Island where they get shat on by seagulls and gnawed on by rats. The mind-blowing "The Fire in Which You Burn" finds Ravi Shankar getting dragged through a vacant lot by a peg-legged midget body-builder, while the devastating battle rhymes of "Vital Nerve" are set atop a shuddering bassline made out of the flatlining cardiographs of all the murdered MCs left in their wake.

Funcrusher Plus isn't all formal experimentation, however. As El-P told *The Wire* magazine, "It was just us talking shit. It was just us trying to find the funniest and most clever ways of saying, 'You suck.'" There are plenty of the one-line mini-epiphanies that are hip-hop's raison d'être, even if they use a slightly more intellectual frame of reference: "My style is *War and Peace*, your shit is just the Cliff Notes"; "Fuckin' with your theology like Darwinism in the Bible Belt"; "Even when I say nothing it's a beautiful use of negative space."

Buried inside the unremitting torrent of largely untranslatable code and forbidding urban Gothic grime, though, is a touching, vulnerable humanity. The stunning "Last Good Sleep" must be the most moving song hip-hop has produced: "He almost killed your mom / If I knew I could have done some-

thing / You'll never see him again / Yeah, but I see him every night / And cover my ears in tears as he beats his fucking wife."

Company Flow perhaps came too close to the brink with this record, and after 1999's instrumental *Little Johnny from the Hospital*, they broke up. El-P started the Def Jux label, which in 2001 released the equally remarkable debut album from Cannibal Ox, *The Cold Vein*. Bloody, dirty, intense (*really* intense), intimidating, tremulous, claustrophobic, but ultimately as inspiring as the sun rising over the Empire State Building, *The Cold Vein* is the album that just might save independent hip-hop from its own worst instincts. Unlike underground university grads like Anti-Pop Consortium and Anticon, Cannibal Ox's Vordul Megilah and Vast Aire aren't arty cats out to wow you with artifice, nor are they beat diggers out to wow you with their dusty artifacts. Instead, *The Cold Vein* unites the street corner and the dorm room, the cipher and the poetry slam, the backpacker and the gat-packer seamlessly. Without even trying, it produces, for whatever it's worth nowadays, the "realest" hip-hop since *Enter the Wu-Tang*.

Vast Aire, who "flow[s] like arachnids on water spouts," is the star, delivering the most vivid descriptions of urban heartbreak and survivalism since Richard Wright: "You were a stillborn baby / Your mother didn't want you, but you were still born/Boy meets world, of course his pops is gone/What you figure/That chalky outline on the ground is a father figure"; "I rest my head on 115/But miracles only happen on 34th." The lyrics are only intensified by El-P's production: a wasteland of percussive rubble and biting, steely synth winds enhanced by a palette of black eyes and bruises, stinging guitars, punch-drunk rhythms, and even the odd, strangely anthemic chorus of Valkyries. At the end, despite (or maybe because of) their unflinching eyes and ears, Cannibal Ox find just enough that stirs the soul to make life worth living; the pigeon, whose life they've spent fourteen songs chronicling, suddenly becomes weightless and fire-proof—a phoenix rising above Harlem's ocean of shit.

by Melissa Maerz

The Coup: Genocide and Juice (Wild Pitch, 1994)

The Coup:
Genocide and Juice

Most rappers insist they're not role models. But if you ask a young hip-hop fan what he wants to be like when he grows up, he's much more likely to mention a mic than a Mike. The Coup's frontman Boots Riley still wants to be a role model, but in a genre where boasting piles of cash scores the most cultural currency, The Coup's 1994 album *Genocide and Juice* makes him an unlikely hero. The self-proclaimed communist proselytizes in a nonchalant tone while delivering incendiary lyrics that condemn the rich, criticize the welfare system, and brag about stealing —all while sounding a little like Too $hort rapping in a Free Winona T-shirt. But he doesn't just do it for street cred: Riley implies that he's redistributing the wealth, making one tiny step toward capitalism's inevitable collapse. And when hip-hop's bling has finally blung, he suggests, The Coup will be right there waiting.

After the explosive 1993 debut, *Kill My Landlord,* which dropped on the heels of 1992's Rodney King–inspired LA Riots, *Genocide and Juice* finds the Oakland group grappling with what has always been their central predicament: The more radical The Coup's lyrical incitements to worldwide rebellion, the less likely they are to bring their message to the very public who could join their army. The album's overly simplistic, bumper sticker polemics sometimes feel too facile, most notably on the violin-laced "Pimps (Free Stylin' at the Fortune 500 Club)," an attack on rap fans from high society. (Who *wouldn't* hate the gluttonous straw man boasting that he sucks down shrimp while you survive on Top Ramen?) But when the tracks are bolstered more by the power of their personal narratives than by their blanket assumptions about the rich, they prove effective rabble-rousers. Pam the Funkstress rolls out 1970s soul on "Fat Cats, Bigga Fish" that could make your lowrider slink away in shame, while Boots scams a bus ride with a stolen pass, steals some unsuspecting pedestrian's wallet, seduces a fast-food worker to get a free hamburger, and ultimately crashes a party overrun with wealthy folk. The song's most important message isn't a revolutionary plot: It's that even communist icons like Riley can actually have a sense of humor.

Delivered with a sad laugh, *Genocide and Juice* rages against corporate bigwigs while educating the record buyers amongst them about what it's like to have your furniture dragged away by the repo man. It suggests to those listeners similarly lacking in resources that somewhere out there is a general mass of people like them, just waiting to be organized. It throws out ornate funk and bass-heavy beats so trance-inducingly catchy that they could serve as jingles for the Black Panthers' televised revolution. Yet the album also hints that the girls working at Burger King are probably more likely to sing rap's equivalent of the American dream—the rags-to-riches Horatio Alger myth—than they are to form a union.

Political rap dates quickly, but *Genocide and Juice* sounds just as prescient a decade later as it did upon its release. The album's subtle storytelling attacks the inextricable link between wealth and power in America, which seems especially appropriate during an era in which imperialism's wickedness can be spelled with a capital Dubya. Perhaps even more so than 2001's controversial post–September 11 release *Party Music*, *Genocide and Juice* points plainly to the consequences of the corporate greed upon which capitalism's structure is based. And even in a time when we're mourning CEOs, we can still critique the system they've helped to create.

by Jeff Chang

Cypress Hill: S/T (Ruffhouse/Columbia, 1991)

Cypress Hill:
S/T

There is no real estate in Los Angeles called Cypress Hill. South of South Central, just off a very flat boulevard called Cypress Avenue in the postindustrial swamp of Southgate—yet another rotting smoghole for youth exiled from the economy of the future—this trio of transplants (Italian, Cubano, and Cubano/Mexicano) invented their hood.

Cypress Hill could have been Anyhood, albeit one transformed by Latinos fleeing *gringo* cold-war bullying south of the Rio or the Keys only to find the same old shit *en el otro lado*. The kind of place where English was broken, jobs were endangered, paranoia was palpable, and the most advanced technology was in the killing hands of the cops. Where the only sane reaction was to act hard and trip hard and sometimes scream, "La lala la lalalalaaaaaa!"

The place that Cypress Hill most resembled, of course, was Chief Darryl Gates's Los Angeles, a sprawling police-state borderland where the hand of the state was permanently pressed upon a baton or a gun or a neck. Brown-skinned peasants swaggered like dukes trying to avoid being Rodney Kinged. At night, they dreamed of jailhouse judgments for corrupt cops. In between, they got high and chased each other in circles—specters and Scooby Doo, y'all.

The celluloid ur-realism of *Wildstyle* weighed heavily on the crew's mind (see "Hole in the Head," "Break It Up," "Something for the Blunted"), particularly the movie's maniacal trickster Rammellzee—from Cypress Hills, Brooklyn—striding across the screen with a hand on the pump of a sawed-off shotgun. When B-Real opened his mouth, his nasal intonation summoned Gangsta Duck beat-bop. So Cypress Hill dissolved the East/West division and became a Hip-Hop Everywhere, where the Wildstyle amphitheater was next to Sister Maggie's weed spot was next to O'Malley's police precinct was next to the Southgate High football locker room was next to Kool and the Gang's rehearsal space was next to the Neighborhood Family set turf was next to Muggs's bedroom studio.

Under B-Real's cinematic eye, the place came alive, sometimes luridly—"I remembah sistah Maggie, breasts were kinda saggy / used to sell me buddha out of fucked-up little baggies"—other times hazily. Muggs's restless bricolage blues always had another corner to turn, another beat to plunder. The sound mimicked a THC high perfectly: as soon as you thought you had grasped the groove, it slipped through and became another. Muggs used scads of found noise, like kids' voices, but often left them inscrutable and indefinite. (Is the schoolyard holler looped in "Real Estate" expressing laughter or terror, affirmation or indiscretion?) B-Real taunted, "You think you know what I'm meaning?"

Later, when they harnessed and streamlined their signifiers, the band would become a cultural phenomenon and an uninteresting product. ("This ain't no exploitation," B-Real said of his blunt-smoking on "Stoned Is the Way of the Walk." No, not yet.) But this self-titled debut—the second inspired West Coast answer to BDP's *Criminal Minded* and a Spanglish response to the first, N.W.A.'s *Straight Outta Compton*—brimmed with importance. If it didn't claim knowledge, it offered street wisdom. Ice Cube's defense was that life was all about bitches and money, but B-Real turned the tables on the prosecution: "Say some punk tried to get you for your auto / Would you call the one-time and play the role model? / No! I think you'd play like a thug."

The Hill was the imaginary real estate they could own. Los Angeles's real hills would never be taken, as rioters learned on April 30, 1992. Pushing north from their hoods at dusk, they found US infantries waiting for them somewhere around Hollywood Boulevard. "When you're up on your hill in your big home / I'm out here risking my dome / Just for a bucket or a fast ducat / Just to stay alive," B-Real said, staring up and waving his fist at the hoods that the riots would never scar. Sometimes all you can take home with you is your hip-hop.

Del: I Wish My Brother George Was Here (Elektra, 1991)
Souls of Mischief: '93 'til Infinity (Jive, 1993)
Casual: Fear Itself (Jive, 1994)

by Lefty Banks

Del:
I Wish My Brother
George Was Here

Souls of Mischief:
'93 'til Infinity

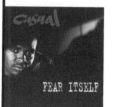

Casual:
Fear Itself

Despite its cosmopolitan reputation, the San Francisco Bay Area is actually one of the most isolated metropolises in America. Travel five hours in any direction and you won't hit another major city; instead, you'll wind up in rural country, sparse desert, or the Pacific's depths. The upside to this seclusion is how the Bay has long been a fertile base for groundbreaking artists, far removed as it is from the record-industry machines in Los Angeles and New York (think Sly Stone, Santana—hell, even E-40).

But despite the success of Too $hort and Digital Underground in the 1980s, the early 1990s were largely a dead zone for Bay Area rappers save for the pimp/players like Spice 1, JT the Bigga Figga, and $hort Dog himself. The scene was similar to the gangsta-dominated Los Angeles landscape prior to Freestyle Fellowship and the Pharcyde. Ironically, Del tha Funkee Homosapien was cousin to one of the biggest gangstas of 'em all—Ice Cube. Unlike his bean pie and malt liquor slingin' relative, Del's irreverent humor made him far closer kin to Digital Underground than Da Lench Mob. Yet contrary to DU and Del's penchant for P-Funk, the funky man's 1991 debut, *I Wish My Brother George Was Here*, was something else entirely.

Compared to the other Bay rappers, Del was in a class by himself. His flow was mercurial, slippery, a slapstick assemblage of syllabic precision that would eventually evolve into brilliant eccentricity. On *I Wish*, he blends superior flow control and a delightfully baffling array of non sequitur boasts. Here's an archetypal winner from "Ahonetwo, Ahonetwo": "I chiseled up a sculpture/to complement my culture/thoughts of silly Nubians is prone to give me ulcers/hanging with the brothers who are tribal in their ways/for this is how I like to spend my days."

Despite the adroit lyricism of songs like "Same Ol' Thing" and "Ya Lil' Crumbsnatchers," what really makes *I Wish* such a remarkable album is how it invites the listener into Del's world. If cousin Cube was busy painting stark pictures of underclass South Central, Del invited listeners to join the low-end, middle-class environs of East Oakland, a mind-state somewhere between the trife life of "Hoodz Come in Dozens" and the idyllic Bay Area portrait of "Sunny Meadowz." For Del, daily threats didn't come from gangbangers or the police, but from freeloading friends ("Sleepin' on My Couch"), sexy gold diggers ("Dark Skin Girls"), and the broke-ass bus system ("The Wacky World of Mass Transit").

A strange element to the album is that Ice Cube, DJ Pooh, and the Boogiemen produce the bulk of it. And while Del handles the Motorbooty funk they dish out with aplomb—*I Wish My Brother George Was Here* is partially a nod to a George named Clinton—the fit seems a little forced at times, especially on P-Funked-out cuts like "Dr. Bombay" and "What Is a Booty?" Del seems to take better to slicker tracks like "Ya Lil' Crumbsnatchers," which borrows a funky dance loop from the Bar-Kays, or the quick-paced "Ahonetwo, Ahonetwo," with its Eddie Harris jazz sample.

Del's future sound—and that of the entire Hieroglyphics family—is caught in these songs and especially in Del's legendary 12-inch B-sides "Burnt" (which introduces the Hiero crew on record) and "Eye Examination" (a Bay Area all-time braggadocio classic). Abandoning the P for a taste of rare groove, Del ups the ante on his innovative lyricism.

By 1993 and 1994, the Hieroglyphics emerged full force, and with Del's *No Need for Alarm*, the Souls of Mischief's *93 'til Infinity*, and Casual's *Fear Itself*, there seemed to be a cascade of crashing waves bringing in new sounds and styles from the Pacific. Just as their Southern affiliates like the Fellowship turned towards the vibe of '70s jazz and soul, the Hieros raided everyone from trumpeter Freddie Hubbard to more obscure artists like local East Bay jazz/rock group Loading Zone. Though the crew had Domino and Jay Biz, impressive producers-at-large, most of the artists produced for themselves and each other, especially Del, Casual, and the Souls' A-Plus. The resultant sound fit on a continuum that defied geography, falling into the tail end of A Tribe Called Quest and Pete Rock's generation of producers. That sound combined with the Hiero's scintillating lyrical aggression meant many in the group could have been confused with East Coast MCs (except that they were largely ahead of the New York massive in this pre-Nas, pre-Biggie era) if it wasn't for their unique Bay Area drawl, slang, and perspective.

Given all this, Del's *No Need for Alarm* should have been a shoo-in as a trend-setting album, but it ends up being the least consistent of the mid-'90s Hiero trio. Del's lyricism hasn't fall off—if anything, he's improved the complexity of his patterns and hands out a barrage of brass-knuckled verbal slaps. But the album is one long fest of disrespect; while the edgier mood has its moments, it easily descends into one-note repetition. The LP sits on the edge of greatness, but ironically, its sole focus makes the album feel decidedly unfocused, and it's never as easy or graceful a listen as you'd want or expect.

Instead, the Souls of Mischief's *93 'til Infinity* captures the Hiero's breakout moment the best with its boundless energy and infectious excitement. Impressively, the four MCs—A-Plus, Opio, Phesto, and Tajai—execute the lyrical equivalent of a four-man weave. On songs like "That's When Ya Lost" the verbal battery is relentless, practically pummeling you into submission as the MCs finish each other's sentences and hand off verses faster than a relay team does a baton. Admittedly, it can be hard to figure out who's who and true aficionados argue over which member of the quartet is the nicest, but all of them flex an incredible, agile flow thatbounces and twists with effortless accuracy. Alone, any one of them would be a contender for greatness—put them together and the Souls are a wrecking crew of freestyling destruction.

There's certainly no shortage of verbal virtuosity here: "93 'til Infinity" is a classic blend of down-home descriptions of girl-watching and bud-smoking, with dashes of braggadocio sprinkled in; "Batting Practice" is pure smash-and-grab; and "A Name I Call Myself" is the Souls' take on mack-adocious strutting. But more than just an endless array of syllable-slinging, the Souls balance the album out with cuts like "Anything Can Happen," a fanciful revenge narrative; "What a Way to Go Out," a well-meaning, though uneven, morality track; and "Live and Let Live," a deceptive selection in which hints of violence are masked by a reflective tone and pacing: "Not a gang-banger, crack-slanger, never done had the rep kid/Yet sweated, frequently/see me and step with intent to kill/spilling your blood for your sins" (Opio).

In contrast to the Souls' explosive lyricism, on *Fear Itself* Casual is more deliberate in his prattle —but no less devastating. The most conventional of the Hiero MCs, Casual is the clear bruiser, the battle rapper eager to eat up any and all competitors. There's a thickness to Casual's voice, a molasses-like grain that makes his brutal verbal inflictions all the more so. His first single, "That's How It Is," is another braggadocio classic, not just from the Hieros, but from Cali in general, with boasts so brazen they stun you into silence: "And you'll run and tell your man, 'Yo, peep this twist,/it's real, try to practice.'/ But the mack is way ahead of ya/instead of ya wack sound,/I'm kicking shit to make MCs back down."

To a degree, Casual suffers from the same one-note tendencies that damage Del's *No Need*, but *Fear Itself* avoids monotony. That's partly due to Casual's charisma; Del's mo' complex, but Casual's more accessible with his swift-kick-to-the-ass disses. But as the last album in the Hiero trio to be released, this album also has the best production. *Fear Itself* eases down from *93 'til Infinity*'s hyperactive pace and finds a solid rhythm mid-tempo, building on sparser productions of splintered drum breaks, meditative melodies, and long, rolling basslines. There's truly impressive feats of beat-making by Casual, Domino, and Del on tracks like the slow-burning "Follow the Funk," the swinging "We Got It Like That," and the surprisingly bright and airy "Thoughts of the Thoughtful."

By 1995, the Hiero reign would end and the crew, en masse, would retreat to a successful—if less spectacular—career on their own independent label. But in the space of two years, the Hieros helped inspire an entire generation of Bay Area artists like the Solesides crew, Bored Stiff, the Dereliks, et al., and joined forces with their LA brethren to fashion a Cali-based conglomerate of lyrical might. '93 didn't quite last to infinity in the way they may have fashioned, but through their enduring influence the Hieroglyphics still have claimed a piece of immortality.

Dr. Dre: The Chronic (Death Row, 1992)
Snoop Doggy Dogg: Doggystyle (Death Row, 1993)

by Oliver Wang

Dr. Dre:
The Chronic

Snoop Doggy Dogg:
Doggystyle

The Chronic was a strange phoenix to rise out of the smoke and ashes of the 1992 LA Rebellion. Whereas Dre's former N.W.A. partner Ice Cube released *The Predator*, an album soaked in I-told-you-this-would-happen self-righteousness, Dre himself always seemed more interested in making ghetto profit rather than being a ghetto prophet. With the exception of *The Chronic*'s "The Day the Niggaz Took Over," which only superficially addresses the chaos of April '92, the album lacks much direct engagement with the politics of urban rebellion. Yet *The Chronic* clearly rides on the Uprising's aftermath, (re)envisioning a new world order led by gangsters and hustlers who, in Dre's imagination, didn't simply survive the riots, but thrived in their wake.

Arguably the most important rap album to ever come out of California (though *Straight Outta Compton* provides heavy competition), *The Chronic* knocked New York off its teetering pedestal and permanently altered the future sound of rap music. Pundits are fond of saying how the album brought gangsta rap full force into white suburbs, but understanding the LP's allure requires more than seeing it as a quintessential gangsta album. *The Chronic* was also a quintessential LA album.

Granted, Dre's LA is a long way from the sun 'n surf imagery that Angeleno anthems typically evoke, yet "Nuthin' but a 'G' Thang" takes its place alongside other classics like the Mamas and Papas' nostalgia-ridden "California Dreaming" and Randy Newman's subtly sardonic "I Love LA." In all these cases, what's being touted is a mythology, a romanticized ideal of what living (and dying) in LA is all about, seeped in a decadent, fabulous fantasy that's long been part of America's fascination with Los Angeles. Just as the Beach Boys' classic "California Girls" came out at the same time as the Watts Riots of 1965, Dre's idealized vision of LA is a response to the burned-out storefronts left behind in '92—an affirmation that his way of life will continue regardless of what Daryl Gates or Rodney King have to say about it.

These ideas get meticulously encoded in the sound that Dre fashions for the album, a hip-hop equivalent to Brian Wilson's fanatical obsessions over the Beach Boys' *Pet Sounds* or Phil Spector's do-or-die recording of Tina Turner's *River Deep, Mountain High*. Compared with the frenetic, raucous energy of Dre's work on N.W.A.'s *Straight Outta Compton* and *Efil4zaggin*, *The Chronic* eases things back, eschewing the iron-fisted funk of the Meters or James Brown and unwinding instead to lavish soul scores inspired by '70s producers like Quincy Jones, Donny Hathaway, and, of course, George Clinton. Dre's key intervention is with those ubiquitous synthesizers that snake their way through songs like "Dre Day," "Nuthin' but a 'G' Thang," and "Let Me Ride" (the album's singles)—it's a sweetly lush sound that interpolates the smog-tinged summertime sunshine into sonic form.

It seems perverse to use a word like "idyllic" to describe the portrait that Dre paints on the album —a world where death and violence is a built-in part of living—but *The Chronic* is undeniably celebratory. The idea of "Let Me Ride"—which sounds like a plea but is effectively a demand—finds Dr. Dre, Snoop Doggy Dogg, and company rolling in their "sweet chariot," a soft-top '64, down palm-lined streets and across a Southland Promised Land of backyard barbecues, gang truce picnics, corner dice games, and bustling swap meets.

Yet, in contrast to this airy, sunny levity, the second half of *The Chronic* is much darker and claustrophobic. If the soaring sound of "Let Me Ride" imagines an open sea of concrete to coast on, the deep, dense drama of songs like "A Nigga Witta Gun" and "Rat-Tat-Tat-Tat" invokes the tense, cramped space of a back alley shoot-out. Moreover, the B-side's two best songs, the posse cuts "Lyrical Gangbang" and "Stranded on Death Row," hit with as much staccato force as any "East Coast" beat, broadening the appeal of *The Chronic* beyond just the slick soul of its better-known hits.

In the process, Dre effectively scores a neo-Blaxploitation soundtrack for the 1990s, tapping into a larger, black cultural continuum as the album recycles the past as it reinvents the present. That's why the gangster, the pimp, and the hustler make up the central iconography on *The Chronic*, going a long way to explain both the album's casual embrace of "Rat-Tat-Tat-Tat"'s violence as well as "Bitches Ain't Shit"'s inexcusable misogyny.

If Dre fashions himself into the modern-day Gene Page, he finds his Leon Haywood in Snoop Doggy Dogg. With his country drawl and easygoing flow, Snoop would seem like an unlikely gangsta candidate, but the relaxed, almost seductive manner in which he talks about gun blasts and pimp smacks makes Snoop seem so damn cool that he can't be expected to break a sweat as a G—it just comes naturally. *The Chronic* introduces a host of rappers, including Daz Dillinger, Kurupt, RBX, and the Lady of Rage (who ironically turns in one of the album's best cameos despite *The Chronic*'s omnipresent sexism). But it's clear from jump that Snoop is top dog over the rest, and his soft-spoken voice is as much a vital part of the album's sound as Dre's studio tweaking.

Snoop's *Doggystyle* isn't as intricate as *The Chronic*, but it's impossible to completely separate one from the other. If *The Chronic* is the buildup, *Doggystyle* is the release, and despite the inclusion of more sinister songs like "Serial Killa" and "Pump Pump," *Doggystyle* is fundamentally a gangsta party album. For tracks like "Gin and Juice," "Tha Shiznit," and "Doggy Dogg World," Dre transforms the daytime glow of *The Chronic*'s grooves into late-night club jams. The genius song is "Ain't No Fun"; its whirring, swirling synths combine with the buzzing basslines and Nate Dogg's crooning falsetto to form a body-hugging funk fabric that is so tight, you barely notice how ignorantly sexist the rhymes are.

Snoop clearly has little care for redemption: he's a gangster and a hedonist and couldn't give a fuck if that bothers anyone as he hustles with style. It's fitting that he chooses to cover Doug E. Fresh and Slick Rick's "La Di Da Di" (entitled "Lodi Dodi" on *Doggystyle*), since both he and Rick share the ability to rhyme with such effortless ease that it hides the complexities of their lyrics underneath a honeyed charm. For example, this evocative verse is from "Murder Was the Case," *Doggystyle*'s most ambitious song about Snoop's existential journey through death, life, and this narrated trip into prison: "Niggaz stare as I enter the center / They send me to a level 3 yard, that's where I stay / Late night I hear toothbrushes scraping on the floor / Niggaz getting they shanks, just in case the war pops off."

There've been many who've blasted and bemoaned *The Chronic* and *Doggystyle*, whether for the unabashed misogyny, the triumph of gangsta mentalities over New School positivity—or simply because they have a distaste for Dre's sound. But the impact of these two albums is above debate. Even ten years later, the indelible image that these albums inspire is of an ageless Dre and Snoop slow-rolling on a bed of funk, floating fingers twisted into a "W," drifting into the sunset of another endless California summer.

by Elizabeth Mendez Berry

Eminem: The Slim Shady LP (Interscope, 1999)

Eminem:
The Slim Shady LP

Hip-hop has long been a haven for the underdog, a utopian space in which society's disenfranchised—mostly young black males—occupy positions of power. But though its heroes don't appear on postage stamps, they do exhibit traditional masculine traits: muscle, confidence, virility. As a white man, Eminem occupies a position of relative privilege in mainstream America, but he's a hip-hop outsider, an insecure peroxide blond pseudopsycho with paranoid tendencies. He describes himself on "Brain Damage" from his 1999 debut, *The Slim Shady LP*, as "a corny lookin' white boy, scrawny and always ornery / 'Cause I was always sick of brawny bullies pickin' on me."

Consider Eminem's career a revenge of the nerd: after years of sucking on the fuzzy end of every lollypop (from his trailer park childhood to his dysfunctional marriage), he's getting back at the world. With his first two albums, Eminem crashes the popular kids' party with guns drawn. Both *The Slim Shady* and *The Marshall Mathers LP*s pack an ante-upping wallop, each incorporating a level of imagery, wordplay, and songcraft seldom seen in the hip-hop world. While he's seldom likeable, it's hard not to root for the artist formerly known as Marshall Mathers. The ninety-eight-pound weakling finally gets to unleash the savage eloquence that he honed while being stuffed inside lockers and upside down into garbage cans. When he tears bad guys to shreds—from grade-school bruisers to holier-than-thou hypocrites—we savor the taste of their blood. But too often, instead of teaching the bullies a lesson, he becomes one himself.

One of the fundamental theories about domestic violence is that people who feel powerless try to counter that feeling by controlling anybody they can. Thus, a man whose boss mistreats him abuses his wife. This vicious cycle may explain Eminem's most significant weakness: When he stops self-flagellating and turns his ire outward, his targets are even lower on the hip-hop food chain than he is. Women in general (with an especially vicious focus on his own wife and mother) and gays, two groups who are rarely passed the mic to strike back, bear the brunt of his well-developed rage. Bad parents also feel the heat. Though he has been described as a renegade by himself and others, Eminem's politics have more in common with John Ashcroft than dead prez, and his blond-haired, blue-eyed looks and prodigious talent, swathed in Dr. Dre's syrupy beats, give his message unusual pop appeal. Disguised in tattoos and obscenities, his Family Values come off as rebellion for the MTV generation.

Eminem has called himself "the new Ice Cube." He's certainly got the ammunition—poor whites are one of the most neglected demographics in America—but Em's work lacks the scathing social commentary that was the method in Cube's madness. On "My Name Is," he offers a mission statement: "God sent me to piss the world off." Not quite the whole world, though. Despite attacking the patriarchy's usual punching bags with zeal, Eminem knows who writes his checks. Dr. Dre is his patron, and the blue-eyed brat is acutely aware of his status as rap's resident alien: he has the most offensive mouth running, but never uses the "N" word. While giving lyrical love to tragic (black) legends like Tupac and Biggie, he disses white rappers and a whole lot of other Caucasians (boy bands, Britney Spears) hard. Most everybody without melanin is

fair game, and Eminem's alter ego, Slim Shady, provides a convenient alibi for his creator to hide behind. According to Eminem, Shady is a sick and twisted individual who is to be feared, but not to be taken seriously. He insulates himself against future lawsuits on the intro to his debut: "Slim Shady is not responsible for your actions / Upon purchasing this album, you have agreed not to try this at home."

Quid pro quo taken care of, the games begin. It's exhilarating to hear Eminem go off the deep end, cussing the whole way down. Tongue is worn either sticking out or lodged deep in cheek. On *Slim Shady*'s "Cum on Everybody" he raps, "I go on stage in front of a sellout crowd and yell out loud, 'All y'all get the hell out now! / 'Fuck rap, I'm givin' it up y'all, I'm sorry,'" to a chorus of "'But Eminem, this is your record release party!'" *Slim Shady*'s "My Fault" is a hilarious rave misadventure. Tripping on everything except his ego, Eminem moans, "I just wanted to make you appreciate nature," as he tries to cope with the mushroom overdose of "a new-wave blond babe with half of her head shaved."

And when he stops taking potshots at sitting ducks (literally: on *The Marshall Mathers LP*'s "I'm Back," he steals Christopher Reeve's legs) and focuses on storytelling, he's unrivaled. *Mathers*'s "Stan" is unforgettable, a stalker tragedy that illustrates Eminem's acute awareness of the image he has created. It's an artfully constructed glimpse at the person hiding behind the middle finger, the aural equivalent of standing in a room full of mirrors. *Slim Shady*'s "Guilty Conscience" is equally artful, but more disturbing: the song is a triple-deckered immorality tale in which Eminem encourages a young male character to rape a fifteen-year-old girl at a rave. While the track is often witty—especially when Eminem starts goading Dr. Dre, here playing the good conscience—its chillingly casual misogyny illustrates Em's troubling the-only-female-I'll-ever-treat-right-is-my-daughter attitude.

Eminem is one of the most agile lyricists in heavy rotation. Serious about his craft, he pushes himself—wordplay improves, cadences evolve, delivery changes up. He never flows the same way twice. But Eminem does not apply the same standard of excellence to his subject matter. There are too few "Stan"s, too many "Kill You"s. And too much whining. Em's self-deprecation is refreshing, but his persecution complex is getting stale. Then again, Eminem does have it hard: he's rich, famous, white, and male.

by Jeff Chang

V/A: Enjoy Records (The Best of) (Hot, 1989)

V/A:
Enjoy Records
(The Best of)

Commercial rap history began with the Sugar Hill Gang's "Rapper's Delight," so rap sounded more like a disco novelty than the sound of the future. But indie R&B labels like Sugar Hill, Winley, and Enjoy—all of which had been nearly crushed by big-production, major-label disco—saw an opening.

In his storied career, Harlem rhythm and blues producer, record seller, and Enjoy label head Bobby Robinson had discovered talents like King Curtis and Gladys Knight and the Pips only to lose them to majors. His business fortune, like the black and brown mecca he called home, was in decline. Yet his office and record shop on 125th Street, just down the block from the Apollo Theater, was only a few train stops away from the ferment of the emerging culture.

As early as 1976, he began noticing hip-hop. His young employees were hip-hop fans, and his son and his nephew were aspiring rappers. When an unrelated set of Robinsons across the Hudson—Sugar Hill's mother-son duo of Sylvia and Joey—outflanked him by releasing "Rapper's Delight," Robinson began haunting Bronx and Uptown hip-hop parties. Youths took him for a cop tracking a perp or a parent looking for a child. But his persistence paid off when he signed two of the scene's hottest acts, the Funky Four + One More and Grandmaster Flash & the Furious Five. He went on to add the Treacherous Three, the Disco Four, and the Fearless Four, not to mention Doug E. Fresh, Kool Kyle, Dr. Ice, and the Masterdon Committee. Between 1979 and 1982, Enjoy's mathematics were unstoppable.

Early recorded rap represented an extended experiment in how to translate a live format into a commercially viable one. Of the early rap indies, Enjoy stands out for both its quantity and quality. During the label's life span, no other cut more singles. And as *The Best of Enjoy* demonstrates, Robinson recognized the strengths of the form. The label's output captured the risk, the musicality, and above all, the exuberance of the young rap scene. Almost all of Enjoy's sides denoted a high-water mark for the still-nascent scene. Robinson's scouts steered him to the scene's innovators and in turn, he gave them what they needed to clarify their vision. Enjoy's ventures into electro with Masterdon Committee's "Funk Box Party" and the Fearless Four's "It's Magic" and "Rockin' It," for instance, were widely imitated. Doug E. Fresh's "Just Having Fun" encapsulates almost the entirety of human beat-box routines in just over five minutes.

If "Rapper's Delight" demonstrated rap's commercial potential, the Furious Five's "Superrappin'" represented its artistic potential. In Melle Mel's words, they were "rapping like hell, making it sound like heaven." Here, at their unreconstructed best on their official recorded debut, the Furious Five balanced unison rhymes and individual lines with verve. They chose to deliver their show-stopping routine. Ironically, they did it sans the Grandmaster, whose solo electronic beat-box drumming was the center of that routine. Instead, Robinson brought in a band to interpolate one of Flash's favorites, the Whole Darn Family's "Five Minutes of Funk." (The Funky Four + One More would also record without their longtime DJ, Breakout.) For these seven minutes (the longer twelve-minute version is not included here), the tension between what rap was—a live performance medium dominated by the DJ—and what it would become—a recorded medium dominated by the rappers—is suspended. History itself seems to be held in place.

Robinson's nephew was the sublimely gifted Gabe "Spoonie Gee" Jackson. Because Robinson hadn't been paying close enough attention, Spoonie had recorded his first record, "Spoonin' Rap," for disco singer/producer Peter Brown's Sounds of New York label. But Robinson captured Spoonie's all-time best, "Love Rap." Unlike "Superrappin'," this was hip-hop as the kids recognized it, as it was heard in the parks, the clubs, and the OJ cabs. Backed only by a steaming, phased drum break by the legendary Pumpkin, Spoonie drops a tale of fast girls and cheap love. "To the beat y'all!" he raps, with an infusion of adrenaline and a tinge of echo.

Before the label faded, Robinson recorded one last classic: the Treacherous Three and Spoonie Gee's "New Rap Language." Kool Moe Dee, LA Sunshine, Special K, and Spoonie Gee had studied and mastered the Furious Five's group dynamics and added quicksilver-tongued, style-destroying, metaphor-drunk skills to this tour de force. The track proved crucial to later rap movements, particularly the following decade's rise of the Freestyle Fellowship and the True School. It also signaled a new stage in the development of rap. The crew turned its gaze "to the south, to the west, to the east, to the north," brimming with the confidence hip-hop would need to jump out of the boroughs and go worldwide. Sylvia and Joey Robinson's Sugar Hill would be the sole surviving label of recorded rap's early years, but *The Best of Enjoy Records* makes the indisputable case that Bobby Robinson's was the most influential.

EPMD:
Strictly Business (Priority, 1988)
Unfinished Business (Priority, 1989)

by Dave Tompkins

EPMD:
Strictly Business

EPMD:
Unfinished Business

Under the name Bobby Jimmy, LA radio personality Russ Parr made a record called "NY/LA Rappers" and made fun of everybody. In the EPMD parody, Parr cut his ess's with some zee's and fell asleep ordering a Big Mac. Customers fell out laughing. Mocking EPMD for the way they hold a piece of steel? The bumper sticker on their 1988 *Strictly Business* debut was "Loungin' in the Danger Zone," but only because Erick Sermon (E Double) and Parrish Smith (PMD) were able to be hard-core without trying too hard. Any bad posturing came from a sunken couch in the boondocks of Brentwood, Long Island. "If you're tired then go take a nap"; serious mumbling from the big guy with a mouthful of Gobstoppers and a floppy hat from golden pond.

Sermon's style *was* EPMD. He sounded like a Sleestack in a leaky beanbag, making the beats seem to slow down, baby, as if time was slipping in his lisp. Meanwhile, Parrish showed you the business end of a microphone because he had juice with Mr. Virgil Sims at Sleeping Bag Records.

Erick and Parrish held the title for one-line choruses. Say it once, grab your nuts, and be out: "You're a Customer," "You Gots to Chill," "It's My Thing." Need your own title? Just go to any verse on an EPMD song. Like the saying goes, "One EPMD line is another man's hook."

While quotes would be snatched off their chest by the dooky load, EPMD were busy yanking their own chains and sampling themselves. On a later album, Erick Sermon thanked himself for being "one of the funkiest niggas in hip-hop." And he was. With much respect to Marley (and much uncredited credit to EPMD coproducer Diamond J), *Strictly Business* might've been New York's first jeep album, lumbering deep in the funk tred. "You Gots to Chill" was first to touch the Ohio slap-funk of Zapp, canceling Bobby Demo's dull "Ounce (Rap)" cover from the early '80s. Roger Troutman's talk-box caught a head code (making "bounce" go whoa), Parrish rocked a Babushka on the single cover, and the video stuck the Jungle Boogie horns in an icehouse.

"It's My Thing" was voted by *The Source* magazine as the Greatest Rap Single of All Time. In '87, when EPMD performed it at Latin Quarter, three big fans fainted when the helicopters started flapping. Once the beat dropped, the oinky bass line meant The Whole Darn Family Had Arrived, and the place was packed tighter than Chubb Rock's lunch box.

Strictly Business also gave us a dance, a DJ cut, and a girl named Jane. "The Steve Martin" was slippin' discs in blue overalls, a herky-jerky move perfected by EPMD's dancer and British cult icon Stezo. With its lurking sharkfin cello, "DJ K La Boss" helped make DJ cuts a standard on rap albums. Then there's Jane, a pretty young thing from the projects who gave EPMD four albums worth of trouble, each time leaving their knees knocked and sending them loping out the door to the beat of "Get Out My Life Woman." Jane's hair went from Anita Baker to Whitney Houston, and by the third episode, to Bobby Brown. Jane became Jay and lived in a hot pink crib with ADT security.

Sermon really gets in touch with his tenderoni side on 1989's *Unfinished Business*, the duo's best album. On "So Wat Cha Sayin'," he slips into a tune-deaf tux tailored to Luther Van's "So Amazing" and goes quiet storm, if only for one time, to a beat world famous for its guitar gurgles, sewer monk moans, and turntable mauling by George Spivey (aka DJ Scratch). Sermon really sings for the golden robe and slippers on "Whose Booty," cracking falsetto teeth while breaking Frederick's "Gentle" promise. ODBs and MF Dooms of the world took note. A rapper could get silky mid-verse and still save scowling face for all the wack bozos.

To EPMD, MCs were accordions and circus clowns. They were NRs (Non-Rappers) in need of "rap alignments," as Sermon's beats amassed enough bass to earn him a rim shop in Atlanta. "Get the Bozack" was named (unintentionally?) after the block party amps cited by Cozmo D ("throwin' down with a rack of Bozacks") on Newcleus's electro smash "Jam on It." Using BT Express guitar stutters for kicks, it could've been Neptunes engineered by Swamp Thing. MZs got Hzed. The James Brown horn stabs of "The Big Payback" were so hard that N.W.A. wore safety glasses in the video.

EPMD's heavy-lidded flow was perfect for "Please Listen to My Demo," which featured a dream in which Parrish was riding high on the ground effects kit of his Benz only to be awoken by a horn toot as their clunker goes chitty on FDR

Drive. But why did E have to get out and push when he made the deal inky beats? Check out the rise and shine of "Demo"'s creamy synth beams as a swervy-nailed siren beckons the duo on to rap fame.

"Please Listen to My Demo" recalls the days before *Strictly Business*—back when the couch had a busted spring, before everybody got on the chuck 'n buckwagon. Engineer Doc Rodriguez remembers that in the studio, Erick and Parrish told him how they were used to spitting in each other's faces with one Radio Shack mic dangling from a steam pipe. That's EPMD. They stepped into the party with old-school amps in their pants and left a permanent, low-end grin on the rap sofa.

EPMD made two more good albums, *Business as Usual* and *Business Never Personal*, before business soured. "Chill" is one of Sermon's best, a dirge led by lumbering cello and drunken brass. "Rampage" had LL and "Headbanger" had their whole damn crew, each of which outspit their mentors. K Solo was a former boxer who stung like a spelling bee. With a knot of Puffs in his nose and an ice slush grill, Reggie Redman Noble looked like he'd been slugged by a boxer, but said nonetheless, "Who cares what rhymes with it as long as the funk pump through my Benz truck." Nobody wanted to hear jack-iggedy from Das EFX after everybody bit their style, plaguing them like Uncle Wiggily's rheumatism. Then there was Keith Murray, a bookish thug with an underutilized belt of "get busy tools."

Murray arrived after EPMD broke up. Once the duo reunited for *Back in Business*, it sounded like a Palmolive handshake with no eye contact. Nor did their solo ventures float, because people just couldn't picture one fishing hat without the other.

by Reginald Dennis

Eric B & Rakim: Paid in Full (4th and Broadway, 1987)

"Think about it—wait, erase your rhyme/Forget it, and don't waste your time."
—Eric B & Rakim, "I Know You Got Soul"

Eric B & Rakim:
Paid in Full

The era that spawned *Paid in Full* may be long gone, but its memory still lingers —especially in the hearts and rhymes of MCs who arrived at the party a decade after the venue was padlocked. You hear it in their fantasies: a pieces-and-bits homage to an age that would have beaten them down and left them for dead had they really tried to walk amongst giants. It's just as well, though—they wouldn't have made it past security.

It was a time of rock cocaine, brick phones, and Iron Mike. Political awareness, trickle-down theories, and shell casings. Thrown mics, sweaty palms, and glazed doughnuts. Real niggas did real things, the kind of things that made legends of few and memories of most. And there, at the center of this hazy, adrenaline-fueled dreamscape—where gutter meets god hood—dwelled the soul controllers: Eric B and Rakim Allah, the President and the Mic Messiah. Two men barely out of their teens. Deep in concentration, serious as cancer, and comfortable as crushed velour.

How many times have you revisited those days? When did "don't nothin' move but the money" and "save it, put it in your pocket for later" become daily words? How long did you stare at the montage of heaven and hell that balanced jewelry, abstract currency, and a check signed by Ronald Reagan with a team photo, grave-yard eyes, and a red stamp of approval from a higher authority? When did this record (seven vocals, three instrumentals) begin to anchor your personal life phi-losophy? To compel you to walk the line between rugged and sharp and crush foes twenty-one at a time?

The legacy of *Paid in Full* endures because we still live in the world, if not the times, that created it. You are reminded of it every time you hear Biggie, Nas, or Jay. It comes back to you in a flash listening to Raekwon's *Only Built 4 Cuban Linx ...*, or Mobb Deep's *The Infamous*, or in the works of countless lesser lights and blown candles. In this respect, Eric B & Rakim remain as much a part of our shared genetic memory as ice grills, ghetto fabulousness, and deferred dreams.

Some believe that the group's legacy came from being so far ahead of their time. Those people are wrong, of course, as they manage to miss the obvious: *Paid in Full* is *not* about the future, it's about what's going on now—*right now*—in the moment. A moment that began generations before a hulking Queens DJ named Eric Barrier ever dreamed that his path would intertwine with that of a magnetic Long Island wordsmith named William Griffin—and will endure long after hip-hop's hall of heroes falls into disrepair.

Paid in Full is about survival, or, better yet, how to live. How to live to see the next day and what to do once you get there. While the ideals expressed are often cloaked in the spiritual—"soul," "knowledge of self," and "actual facts"—Eric B & Rakim are nothing if not creatures of the real world, never forgetting that constant hand-to-hand exchange of goods and services makes the world go 'round.

But more than just a shallow means of keeping score, Eric B (a four corner hustler if there ever was one) and Rakim (the consummate master planner of the Five Percent Nation) know that wealth is simply a tool for the pursuit of true happiness. Money holds no dominion over the truly enlightened, which is why it flows so easily into their pockets. And even without cash in hand, Eric and Ra are still holding heavy because in the end, the only wealth that matters is the kind that no one can take from you.

This lesson, however, seems to be lost on so many of hip-hop's modern-day imitators and cultural scavengers. You can drive the car, wear the jewelry, cash the check, and practice the swagger, but unless you are building on something that is already there, worthwhile, and inside of you, it will never ring true. That's why Eric B & Rakim have stood so far above so many for so long. They are the standard: they know their value and so do we, which is almost as important. We are all gold coins, but what matters most is when we were minted; 1987 was a good year, but only because men like Eric and Ra made it so. They seized the moment and made those days mean something. And in that moment they became immortal, ensuring that they will never be men out of time.

When you hold that crown, you never have to sweat the small details. You never have to look to see who's gaining, or choose between street cred and talent, or be diminished by fear and insecurity. You will never spend your time wishing you were someplace or someone else. And most important of all: You will never have to ask yourself tragic questions like *Can I live?* or tell yourself to *Start punchin' niggas in they face just for living.*

No. Because to do so would mean admitting you are not in control, that someone else determines the course of your life. And that is no way to exist, for we were put here to be much more than that. We have to find life where we can, and live *in* and *for* the moment every day of our lives. If we don't, then we are committing the worst of crimes: wasting time. And time is the only thing we can't buy or get back or re-create.

We only get one shot at this.

No mistakes allowed.

Freestyle Fellowship:

by Oliver Wang

To Whom It May Concern... (Sun, 1991; Beats and Rhymes, 1999)

Freestyle Fellowship:
To Whom It May
Concern...

Like Prince's infamous *Black Album* or Bob Dylan's *Royal Albert Hall* bootleg, the debut of LA's Freestyle Fellowship, *To Whom It May Concern ...*, falls into the category of albums oft raved about but rarely heard. Released on the tiny independent Sun Music imprint in 1991, the album was rumored to have only existed on three hundred vinyl and five hundred cassette copies—a miniscule number by any stretch of the imagination. Yet the album stands as one of the most influential LPs ever released on the West Coast, the fire starter for practically the entire California underground movement in the 1990s and beyond.

It's hard to imagine how such an arguably obscure album could have such an effect, but one needs to appreciate the time and place of the Freestyle Fellowship's emergence. LA's underground community faced the juggernaut of N.W.A., Ice Cube, and like-minded gangsta acts virtually defining what anyone knew about the West Coast. Ironically, despite their boho cachet, the Fellowship exuded the same blustering black masculine bravado inherent among the gangsta clique, but handed down verbal pistol-whippings rather than fantasized drive-bys. They claimed the same South Central roots, but funneled the fury and frustrations of their physical space into the mental space of lyrical imaginations as expansive as the Southland's sprawl.

Honed in freestyle ciphers held in- and outside of the famed Good Life Café, lyrics by Aceyalone, All in All, Mikah 9, P.E.A.C.E., and Self Jupiter countered reality rap's domination with an insurgent virtuosity, raining down complex rhyme schemes and caustic verses like brimstone. As they spell out on "We Will Not Tolerate," "We are not your O-R-D-I-N-A-R-Y R-A-P-P-E-R N-*-G-G-E-R-S." Equally provocative is *To Whom*'s "Sunshine Men," a not-so-subtle dig at New York rappers who tried to ball out the West only to have their cards pulled by the Fellowship. Most memorable is Mikah 9's stunning rhyme marathon "7th Seal." The song kicks off with chaotic guitar riffs only to break down into a funky congo rhythm over which Mikah

9 warns, "Be advised they'll come/Be advised they'll come in/Be advised they'll come/In a pure, black whirlwind." The metaphor seems apt, as Mikah and the rest of his Fellowship laid waste to their contemporary hip-hop landscape and reshaped it in their own chaotic image. They exemplified what photographer/author Brian Cross (aka B+) has called Cali's "post-gangsta" moment, and it's easy to see how the Fellowship would be the catalyst behind everything from the Pharcyde to Solesides/Quannum to Jurassic 5 to Stones Throw, etc.

If their verbal craft took the Fellowship into uncharted regions, so did their music. With LA still in the throes of Dr. Dre and Sir Jinx–engineered funk blasters, the Fellowship took a page from the beat diggers and pulled out a treasure trove of eclectic samples instead. For example, Billy Joel's piano strains accent P.E.A.C.E.'s bludgeoning "For No Reason"; the JBs' slick, thick basslines from "More Peas" powers "Physical Form"; and the Fellowship loop up Grant Green's hyperactive keyboard play for "Here I Am." Curiously, many of these same beats would later be associated with artists like Xzibit, Cypress Hill, and Public Enemy, but they all followed on the Fellowship's heels.

Like the snowflake that sets off the avalanche, *To Whom It May Concern …* bulldozed a path that led others to what is possible when you simply give license to your own creativity, no matter how unconventional it is. Most importantly, the album valorized independence at a time before the concept had become cliché, inspiring an entire generation of artists to follow its lead. In a very real way, *To Whom It May Concern …* has perhaps been the biggest small album that hip-hop has ever known.

Fugees: The Score (Ruffhouse/Columbia, 1996)
Wyclef Jean: The Carnival (Sony/Columbia, 1997)
Lauryn Hill: The Miseducation of Lauryn Hill
(Sony/Columbia, 1998)

by Ernest Hardy

Fugees:
The Score

Wyclef Jean:
The Carnival

Lauryn Hill:
The Miseducation
of Lauryn Hill

Anyone who listened to the Fugees' debut album, *Blunted on Reality*, when it dropped in 1994 can be forgiven for thinking the group didn't have much of a future. Although there are strong glimmers of the brilliance that was to come from Clef and Lauryn (Pras really was the Harpo Marx of the trio—or, more accurately, should have been), the overall disc is shrill and patently false, blunted on posturing. It plays as though Digable Planets decided to front and come off like Onyx, offering up social consciousness and hood reportage that feels secondhand and contrived in its attempts to be hard-core. There's little in the way of real individuality or interesting artistry.

In contrast, 1996's *The Score* is a jaw-dropping revelation of both skills (song-writing, performance, production) and expansive artistic vision. The record succeeds because it lets the group tap into the essence of who its members are: three young Black Americans deeply influenced by a wealth of sounds and musical genres (rap, jazz, pop standards, reggae, blues, folk, R&B) as well as the social and political realities that shaped the world around them. The overall tempo has been dropped a couple of notches from that of *Blunted*—braiding in those reggae and dub influences to fantastic effect—and so has the tendency toward pointless aural assault. In becoming more measured, in offering more considered music, the trio now truly comes hard, both intellectually and with a more nuanced sound aesthetic. They kill us softly with their songs.

On the sparse "How Many Mics," with its prominent, neck bone–relaxing beat, the rappers press hard and close into the microphone, creating an effect of warm immediacy for rhymes that ride front and center over the musical bed. The bravura here isn't merely that of machismo or conventional hip-hop swagger; it is rooted in the confidence to speak in smoothly modulated tones and cadences. Their own vocal idiosyncrasies—throaty rasps, sardonic line readings, honey-coated singing—come to the foreground, announcing their style to the world in a way that *Blunted* did not. That tack makes genuine art out of what is, in essence, a standard rap song sent to slay wack rap emcees while boasting of the Fugees' own prowess, as in Lauryn's verse, "Plus you use that loop over and over / Claiming that you got a new style, your attempts are futile, oooh child / You're puerile, brain waves are sterile."

The track "Zealots" springs its beats and rhymes out of an intro/overture that's lifted from the pop staple "I Only Have Eyes for You," holding on to the classic melody even while transforming it into a state-of-the-'90s sonic essay. The group's moving cover of Bob Marley's "No Woman, No Cry" not only pays tribute to a musical hero, but also foreshadows both Clef and Lauryn's future solo work. Sly & Robbie remixed the hit single "Fu-Gee-La" for a CD bonus track, but the influence of the legendary producers actually sprawls all over the disc, where grooves that are paradoxically dense and sparse act as the foundation for tautly written songs. Additionally, the between-song skits (a now painfully clichéd feature in rap) are fully and richly integrated into the overall vision of the CD.

It was the cover of Roberta Flack's "Killing Me Softly" that scorched the Fugees into mainstream consciousness. But the success turned out to be a mixed blessing. On the strength of massive airplay for the track, suburban housewives, slaves to American Top 40 radio, and bourgeois Negroes all flocked to *The Score*, making it a huge, unexpected pop hit. But many of those folk were baffled by what they encountered: lyrics that dealt with police brutality, studio thugs, and far-flung journeys into the internal worlds of Afro-America—its youth, its artists—awaited anyone who slipped the disc into a player. The album was often greeted with bafflement or resentment by mainstream shoppers who merely wanted their R&B reupholstered in new sounds, not attached to any larger political or cultural statements.

Clef's 1997 solo debut, *The Carnival*, refined, broadened, and sharpened the cultural Cuisinart formula of *The Score*. (He also managed to keep in check the ego, the posing, and the smugness that would deeply mar his next two CDs.) Hip-hop culture blankets the globe; rap music is now *the* music of the world. Clef showed how both are indebted to various musics and cultures from all over the planet. He cast his net from the traditional "Guantanamera" to his own lushly orchestrated, folk-inflected ballad "Gone Till November," and then reached down to capture the feel of old-school basement parties. There's a joy in the overall record that comes from the freedom of being unbridled, of exercising every aspect of one's being—silly, reflective, sexy, and political sides—and knowing that those qualities don't have to be rigidly compartmentalized or humorlessly policed. And this is a record that underscores how important sequencing and context are. As a single, "Tryin' to Stay Alive," which is centered on a sample of the Bee Gees disco classic "Staying Alive," was corny and irrelevant. But as part of *The Carnival*'s larger journey, the track is funny and telling; in its cheesy groove is a reminder of its creator's many dimensions.

When Lauryn dropped *Miseducation* in 1998, the pop and hip-hop worlds were both starved for antidotes to a host of MTV- and BET-fueled ills: the bling! bling! materialism that had infected rap; the wigs, weaves, and cosmetically lightened skin of black women (and the regressive fetishizing of all women, period) in both music videos and the larger domains of popular culture; and music that had nothing to say except shop, fuck, and then shop some more. Lauryn—dark-skinned, full-lipped, capped with dreadlocks, and impossibly beautiful—came with words that spoke to both romantic and political liaisons in the here and now that are too often defined by greed, spiritual corruption, and general ill will. A lot of critics accused her of preachiness or humorless self-righteousness. Much of that response, however, was due to the reflexive "Shut up, nigger, and dance" mentality that still runs deep in "mainstream" (i.e., white) America's relationship to black art and black artists, particularly those who deal seriously with the shittier realities of life in America for a lot of black folk. (Unfortunately, hip-hop has not put nearly the dent in that dynamic that it could have or should have given its twenty-year presence as a factor in the culture game. The reactions of the media to more outspoken or "conscious" black rappers is itself a telling reminder of not only the gaps and differences in perception between "black" and "white" America, but also the arrogance and ignorance with which black art is routinely critiqued under the guise of "objectivity.")

But how could anyone who wasn't tone deaf miss the humor in "Doo Wop (That Thing)," a scathing but often hilarious examination of the gender wars (the blame is assigned equally to both sides, with male *and* female foibles being called out) set against full-bodied production that featured prominent piano riffs, blaring horns, and street-corner harmonies? How could they not pick up on the giddiness that all but spills from the grooves in "Every Ghetto, Every City," Lauryn's paean to her childhood in New Jersey? Those are crucial layers in a disc that veers from the verbal beat-down delivered on "Lost Ones" (which, like many of the tracks, flips easily back and forth between large-scale social critique, unflinching assessment of the dire state of rap, and brusque response to an unfaithful lover) to the beat-driven, emotionally raw ballad "Ex-Factor" (which is as perfect a song as has been crafted in the last decade). There's also "Nothing Even Matters," the shimmeringly erotic duet with D'Angelo; "To Zion," a love song to her infant son, in which Carlos Santana sprinkles effervescent guitar over marching drums; and "Tell Him," a song of faith and devotion that seamlessly marries the secular and the spiritual.

It's true that *Miseducation* is two or three songs too long, and the self-consciously cute between-song interludes are just annoying. But the unfounded, knee-jerk backlash that eventually rose up around both Lauryn and the record can't obscure the fact that the disc is one of the most perfect hybrids of rap and R&B that has yet been created. In its stellar songwriting, heartfelt singing, career-best rapping, and finely rendered production, *Miseducation* announced the arrival of an all-to-rare entity in modern music: a real artist.

Gang Starr:

Step in the Arena (Chrysalis, 1990)
Daily Operation (Chrysalis, 1992)

by Chairman
Jefferson Mao

Gang Starr:
Step in the Arena

Gang Starr:
Daily Operation

When critical conversation turns to the subject of hip-hop's greatest ensembles, Gang Starr isn't usually awarded any practical consideration by the rap cognoscenti. Ever the career underdogs, the group is inevitably outshined by the long list of more pioneering, more successful, and more glamorous outfits that have entered the pop consciousness. Yet there's probably no single act that's exerted as strong an influence on contemporary grassroots/underground/independent rap music than the duo of Guru and DJ Premier. Four out of five Dilated Peoples fans agree: Gang Starr be one of the best yet; a partnership of unparalleled durability that continues to inspire aspiring hip-hop preservationists and make everyman rap music for everyday folk wary of what they're ear-fed on commercial radio every day.

Step in the Arena and *Daily Operation*, Gang Starr's second and third LPs, are the group's twin peaks, the records on which the pair's self-described reputation as "dedicated ministers of underground sounds" was originally built. They are beautifully constructed programs, ones that flow seamlessly together as if of one piece, balancing message, muse, and menace like few albums of the genre. For their time, the albums are progressive enough to satisfy free-spirited Native Tongues devotees seeking constant elevation, and brawny enough to bump bragging writes and crime-rhyme yarns featuring, say, a Just-Ice or Kool G Rap. For every edutainment-minded primer like "Form of Intellect" or scathing institutional indictment like "Conspiracy," there's an "Ex Girl to the Next Girl" (a wry account of female hijinks), a "Take Two and Pass" (a blunt endorsement of herbal recreation), or battle-eager lyrical challenges like "Flip the Script" or "Check the Technique" to maintain the ghettocentricity and prevent the rhetoric from running unchecked.

Occasionally, as with *Arena*'s lead single, "Just to Get a Rep," the dichotomy of Gang Starr's approach merges within one brilliant composition. Here, Guru's vivid narrative follows a stick-up kid's brutal pursuit of an unsuspecting victim, relaying the play-by-play in a detached tone that entirely avoids coming off as didactic. Perfectly set against Premier's sample of Jean-Jacques Perrey's moody moog synth staple "E.V.A.," it's the quintessential Gang Starr moment. (Strangely, the LP version deletes the song's conclusion in which the music mournfully comes to a screeching halt at the story's climax; the superior 12-inch single version is available on 1999's retrospective *Full Clip: A Decade of Gang Starr*.) *Operation*'s "Soliloquy of Chaos," on the other hand, juxtaposes indulgence and ignorance. It sets out as a celebration of crew comradery ("five carloads deep," forties and blunts in hand) and the excitement of performing before a live audience when suddenly, in an all too familiar turn of events, random violence erupts, forcing a show abort. "Did you come to see my show or the stupid nigger playoffs?" Guru asks the knuckleheads that threaten the prospects of this and any other hip-hop concert in a disarmingly sincere plea for peace.

But Guru most neatly encapsulates Gang Starr's thoughtfulness and street savvy in a few lines on *Arena*'s closer, "The Meaning of the Name": "[Gang Starr is] bringing beams of light like the colors in a prism / Or reflections through a spectrum / And all those soft silly suckers, I'ma wet them / In other words, destroy, boy / And then claim my fame."

Unfortunately, fame proved elusive. Despite their obvious merits, neither of these albums managed to go gold. In *Operation*'s case, the group's timeless club smash "DWYCK," featuring Nice & Smooth, was a non-LP B-side that blew up unexpectedly and without an album to support it. (It was later included on the uneven *Hard to Earn*.)

With the additional unfortunate luck of releasing their finest albums during one of hip-hop's most fertile periods, recognition from within the ranks of the emerging rap press proved equally evasive. Both *Arena* and *Operation* garnered a rating of just three and a half mics on *The Source* magazine's widely read "Record Report." That both albums have eventually come to epitomize for many the sound of undiluted New York hip-hop at its best comes as no small victory considering the group's previous dismissal in other critical circles as a novelty-ish "jazz-rap" act in the wake of the Charlie Parker–sampled "Words I Manifest" and the "Jazz Thing" single from the soundtrack to Spike Lee's *Mo' Better Blues*. (Adding further irony to their ultimate acceptance is the fact that both Guru and

Premier were, of all things, out-of-towners—from Boston and Prairie View, Texas, respectively—who'd relocated to New York to pursue their hip-hop dreams.)

Preem's impact as a producer wouldn't be fully felt until after the release of these records. (His minimalist track for Jeru the Damaja's 1993 single "Come Clean" set off an astounding series of collaborations with KRS-One, Nas, Notorious B.I.G., Jay-Z, and many others.) But within the grooves of *Arena* and *Operation*, his genius is nonetheless evident. His sage sequencing instincts provide *Arena* with a unique ebb and flow, utilizing interludes and compact two-minute tunes to break up the longer songs. The jazz samples may have been consciously eschewed, but Preem proves himself capable of pillaging sources as diverse as the JBs, Delfonics, Soul II Soul, and even MOR pop singer Leo Sayer with equally enticing results. *Operation* exhibits his ear for truncated loops on "Ex Girl" and "Soliloquy," reinvents the posse cut by switching up the track for each emcee on "I'm the Man" (featuring Jeru and Lil' Dap of Group Home), and demonstrates expert beat- and sample-chopping skills on the vindictive "Take It Personal" (a style Premier would make a standard production practice and that others would emulate for years).

Gang Starr would finally enjoy a taste of the commercial success it long deserved several years later in 1998 with the gold-certified *Moment of Truth*, a supreme effort that courageously stuck to the group's creative guns at a time when gritty, genuine, gimmick-free hip-hop not of the Bad Boy or synth-dominated, Swizz Beats–produced variety was becoming an endangered species. In fact, rife with Gang Starr standards like "You Know My Steez," "Above the Clouds," and "The Rep Grows Bigga," *Moment* might easily be considered the equal of *Arena* or *Operation* save for one consideration which tips the scales in favor of its predecessors: Collectively, *Step in the Arena* and *Daily Operation* represent the blueprint not only for *Moment*, but for much of what many folks in this day and age consider "real hip-hop" in general. So heed the wisdom of the JanSport-clad crowd and praise these purists. As a Nice man once proclaimed, Gang Starr has gots to be the sureshot.

Geto Boys: We Can't Be Stopped (Rap-a-Lot, 1991)
Scarface: Mr. Scarface Is Back (Rap-a-Lot, 1991)

by Jon Caramanica

Geto Boys:
We Can't Be Stopped

Scarface:
Mr. Scarface Is Back

At the dawn of the '90s, Southern rap didn't command much attention outside of the antics of the filthy Luther Campbell and his 2 Live Crew cronies. Indeed, West Coast rap had only just begun to assert itself in the face of New York's hegemony, so to many, the rise of Houston as a vital hip-hop center went unnoticed until Rick Rubin caught on to the self-produced, self-titled 1990 debut of the Geto Boys—Scarface, Bushwick Bill, and Willie D—and reached out to the group, recording some new material with them and releasing an alternate version of the record called *Grip It! On That Other Level* on his Def American imprint. Houston was finally on the map, and it wasn't pretty. Thanks to a song dealing with necrophilia, Rubin had to seek alternate distribution for the record, and the Geto Boys became unlikely free speech pioneers.

On their next album, 1991's *We Can't Be Stopped*, the newly politicized Geto Boys came out swinging. On the title track, which opened the record, rap's pariah poster boys let it be known just how deeply they frowned on their critics. The hyperactive Bushwick Bill asks, "Can you believe those hypocrites would distribute Guns 'n' Roses and not our shit? / And they say we're a racist act." And in a statement to make the ACLU proud, Willie D warns, "Keep lettin' the government dictate what you hear / Next they'll put stickers on your ear."

In keeping with their brash attitude, the Geto Boys made few lyrical compromises on this album. "Chuckie" was as vividly gruesome as anything the group had yet done, and "Another Nigger in the Morgue" was as violent. Balance came in the form of "Fuck a War," an endearingly bizarre anti–Desert Storm rant by Bushwick Bill, and "Trophy," Willie D's unchecked fire about the Geto Boys' unrequited quest for recognition.

But the album's unquestioned emotional center was "Mind Playing Tricks on Me," one of rap's most psychologically intricate moments to date. Willie D is being followed by an unknown assailant: "… is it that nigga last week that I shot? / Or is it the one that I beat for five thousand dollars? / Thought he had 'caine, but it was Gold Medal flour." Bushwick Bill imagines he and his boys are running wild through the streets on Halloween, stealing trick-or-treat bags and attacking an oversized foe: "… we triple-teamed on him / … / The more I swung the more blood flew / Then he disappeared and my boys disappeared too / Then I felt just like a fiend / It wasn't even close to Halloween / It was dark as fuck on the streets / My hands were all bloody from punching on the concrete."

The Geto Boys may have sounded of one mind on this song, but the fractiousness within the group was already beginning to show on this second album. The majority of the songs were actually solo tracks—each member had about three—and by this time, Scarface was already being acknowledged as the group's true poet. It was inevitable that he would explore a solo career, and he did later the same year with *Mr. Scarface Is Back*. With a flow as aggressive as Ice Cube's and music that approximated an up-tempo version of Too $hort's trunk funk, Scarface proved a formidable soloist. His standard thug routine was well honed by this point. "Good Girl Gone Bad" is a detailed tale of the drug life, and "Murder by Reason of Insanity" takes thuggish bravado to its logical end: "Brothers like me are making mortuaries rich."

For most rappers this would have been ample range, but Scarface was already beginning to shape the persona he would carry with him for the next decade and beyond. He was the penitent thug, a melancholy hustler. In his world, no actions came without consequences, no misstep without an intense psychic burden to match. On "Diary of a Madman," he comes unhinged: "I try to talk to my dad, but my old man ignores me / He says I'm delirious / And I drink too much, so he doesn't take me serious / But little does he know I'm really losing it / I got a head, but ain't no screws in it." Family pain continues on "Born Killer": "My momma did her part / But it ain't her fault that I was born without a heart / In other words, I'm heartless, duke / I don't love me, how the fuck I'ma love you? / That's right, you guessed it / I'm legally insane, marked manic depressive / I'm takin' all types of medication / To keep me out the mood of premeditation."

In these songs, Scarface did what no gangster had yet attempted: show the internal tragedy that underlies all of hip-hop's harsh fantasies (or realities). He was the first to humanize gangster rap and in so doing, proved its viability and diversity as an art form. It was also a vision that would sustain him. While most of his contemporaries have long since fallen by the wayside—his Geto Boys partners included—Scarface has matured into the grandfather of the genre. Thanks to his commanding presence and continual self-examination, he's been able to evolve with the times and still remain utterly relevant, age notwithstanding. He's set the bar cruelly high for younger generations of kids who think they know, but have no idea.

Grandmaster Flash & the Furious Five:
Adventures on the Wheels of Steel (Sequel Records, 2002)

by Jeff Chang

**Grandmaster Flash
& the Furious Five:**
Adventures on
the Wheels of Steel

Time—and a large army of sociologists and remote-control critics—remembers Grandmaster Flash for a rap he didn't write. Released in the hot summer of 1982, just as the Reagan recession peaked, "The Message" touched a nerve. The platinum-selling single seemed to capture the despair of the ghetto, where half of the youths were unemployed and living conditions and police brutality had only worsened since riots of the 1960s.

But the record—written by Sugar Hill house band percussionist Ed "Duke Bootee" Fletcher clearly under the influence of "Red" (Black Uhuru's reaction to the violence-torn, economically ravaged Jamaican landscape) and sealed by an old verse Melle Mel had written for one of the crew's very first singles—was really the beginning of the end for Grandmaster Flash & the Furious Five. Over time, the song has eclipsed Flash's profound contributions to twenty-first-century pop.

After witnessing Kool Herc spin breaks and Pete DJ Jones create seamless remixes of dance tracks in Mitchell Park in 1973, the teenage Flash retreated to his bedroom to theorize what he had seen. He emerged with the "Quick Mix" theory, a way of thinking that not only predicted scratching (which Flash's precocious protégé Grand Wizard Theodore would perfect), but made possible a whole new understanding of the b-beat mix.

Herc had the sound system and Bam had the records, but Flash had the scientific mind and the mixing skills to craft the music into something both raw enough to attract a hard-core audience and polished enough to appeal to outsiders. Flash advanced block party rocking toward turntablism by isolating and breaking down DJing's atoms, then transforming it into a high-performance art. The results were re-created to great effect on Strut Records' 2002 release, *The Official Adventures of Grandmaster Flash*. Both of turntablism's cults—scratch-and-cut technics and battle-drill visual glitz—find their roots in Flash and his protégés' innovations.

Fortunately for hip-hop, his audiences didn't get it at first. So Flash added Keith "Cowboy" Wiggins as an emcee, who would become one of the best hype men in rap history (again, see *The Official Adventures*) and the cornerstone of the Furious Five. By 1979, after "Rapper's Delight," the South Bronx block party scene that Flash and the Furious Five had dominated was dissipating as the core audience grew up and went to Harlem to seek out DJ Hollywood and Eddie Cheeba's more sophisticated rap parties. Flash, who had been turning down record deals, now changed his mind.

But the early rap industry—with its chronic fear of music publishers—had no place for a DJ other than to dictate to house bands how to best mimic turntable routines. Flash's rappers—who were by now unquestionably the best group in New York City—moved to the center stage. Signing to Sugar Hill further limited Flash's influence over his own group, as Sylvia Robinson took a close interest in shaping the act's future.

Flash would make one more bold statement. "The Adventures of Grandmaster Flash on the Wheels of Steel," released in 1981, will always stand as the prototype for recorded and performance turntablism: it was the quantum mechanics to the Quick-Mix theory of relativity. But its torque-driven wizardry also pointed to a bygone time. When Flash worried that "The Message" would alienate his core party audience, Robinson released the record under his name anyway. While Flash's name signified hip-hop's past, rap was hip-hop's future.

Flash developed a side career, providing the iconic face and skillful hands as hip-hop moved first to the desegregated downtown art/punk nightclubs (a period captured on Essential/ffrr's *The Essential Mix*) then on to the international music tabloids. But Robinson's focus on making Melle Mel into rap's first superstar changed the Furious Five's internal dynamics and by 1983, the group had split into two competing camps—both called the Furious Five.

Flash's post–Sugar Hill career was disappointing, and no definitive record of Grandmaster Flash & the Furious Five exists. The three-CD *Adventures* import comes the closest, collecting all the brilliant early Sugar Hill singles: "Freedom," "The Birthday Party," "The Message," "It's Nasty," and even a first (horribly mastered) version of "Super Rappin'." With Duke Bootee stepping up his music- and lyric-writing in the aftermath of Flash, there are other great tracks: "New York, New York" and "Message II (Survival)." But after "White Lines," the slide is long and depressing.

Here's hoping someone will find the heart and the money to pull it all together—the block party and club tapes of the early routines (like the Bronx River Community Center bootleg recording of the beat-box classic "Flash to the Beat," probably the best Flash & the Five performance ever captured); the early singles ("Superappin'" on Enjoy and "We Rap More Mellow," performed as "The Younger Generation" to avoid contractual issues); and a generous culling of the Sequel set—and create a collection that serves musical justice to these deserving giants.

by Allen Gordon

Ice Cube: Death Certificate (Street Knowledge/Priority, 1991)

Ice Cube:
Death Certificate

For all his brazen gangsterisms as a member of N.W.A., Ice Cube's solo career moved him further away from pontificating the culture, mores, and mythology of Los Angeles street life. That process began with 1990's Bomb Squad–produced *AmeriKKKa's Most Wanted*, where Ice Cube took his cues from Public Enemy and redefined political rap in the process. The argument was still very gangsta, yet savvy enough to articulate the social politics of the neighborhood in ways that don't make the rounds in civic, state, or federal congressional meetings.

Ice Cube's commitment to progress is always focused, but he is noncommittal on utopian ideas of Black struggle and nationalist rhetoric. That's where he wins. Ice Cube stands here as a symbol of the uneducated and disenfranchised young Black man awakening to white supremacy and its relationship to his social condition. If this realization began with *AmeriKKKa's Most Wanted*, Ice Cube nailed its apogee on 1991's *Death Certificate*. Having adopted much of the philosophy from his new association with the Nation of Islam and Minister Khalid Muhammad, Ice Cube would spout the fifty-year-old separatist philosophy through the more palatable language of the average street person. Where Ice Cube helped create the image of the apathetic "nigga" with N.W.A., he would now deconstruct and present the origins of the many downtrodden archetypes he previously rapped about.

Divided into a Death Side and a Life Side, *Death Certificate* was a conceptual work that attempted to kill the "nigga" mentality his earlier work reflected in order to give birth to a new culturally and community-minded "Black man." To this end, Ice Cube examines white supremacy, Black pathology, and other factors behind the post–Civil Rights era disenfranchisement of LA's Black youth. There are moments of levity on the album: "Doing Dumb Shit," Cube's tongue-in-cheek look back on his childhood; "Color Blind," the feel-good, let's-all-get-together anthem; and "No Vaseline," Cube's viciously hilarious return volley at his former N.W.A. peers. But when it comes to Cube's main laundry list of political and social issues, *Death Certificate* straddled no fences, evenly scathing all groups and governing systems Ice Cube deemed exploitative of the Black community.

The Death Side begins with a funeral procession, symbolizing the demise of the "nigga," then launches into "The Wrong Nigga to Fuck With," a tirade that charges the US government, LAPD chief Darryl Gates, and Los Angeles Raiders owner Al Davis with crimes of abuse, slavery, and exploitation. As he does on much of *Death Certificate*, Cube here foreshadows the LA rebellion that would take place a year later, his boiling anger reflective of a general mood that was waiting to explode. "Horny Lil' Devil" and "I Wanna Kill Sam" also vent anger about slavery and white supremacy using language equally as abusive as "nigger." It wasn't meant to include all white people, but it doesn't exactly differentiate between them, either.

The same can be said for Asians on "Black Korea," where Ice Cube uses Koreans and the terms "chop suey," "Oriental one-penny counting motherfuckers," and "Jap" as the archetype for Asian storeowners (which also includes the Vietnamese, Chinese, Japanese, and Cambodians) in Black communities. The song, which incited claims of racism and a short-lived boycott of *Death Certificate*, explored how storeowners discriminated against and were suspicious of Black patrons. "Black Korea" didn't try to improve the relationship between the two communities more than it threatened that the establishments it referenced would be burned down if the customer profiling didn't come to an end—another lyric turned prophecy on April 29, 1992.

If Ice Cube was critical of non-Black Americans, he was even more ruthless in his indictment of the Black community. Los Angeles gangs are held accountable for franchising crack cocaine and gang violence to Black neighborhoods across the country on "My Summer Vacation." The moral of Ice Cube's tale ends with gang members becoming slaves in the hostile California penal system, a theme that also serves as the backdrop for "Alive on Arrival," which speaks to the lethal folly in forging friendships with genocidal drug pushers and gang members. "A Bird in the Hand" is the only song to absolve the drug dealer; Ice Cube tells the story of an economically disenfranchised young father in Bush the First's America looking to justify the "quick buck" as a pusher.

On the surface, "Look Who's Burnin'" and "Givin' Up the Nappy Dug Out" seem like simple sexcapade stories, but more telling is the moralizing about sloppy safe sex practices and intraracial classism. The latter song uses a suburban Catholic girl's deviant sex acts with inner-city boys as a way to critique the middle-class belief that moving out of the Black community and acquiring a better education is supposed to provide immunity from the "sickness" of associating with Blacks. Cube revels in exploding that falsehood as he relates to the main character's father what his pride and joy has been up to.

Unlike his previous solo album, Ice Cube overpowers the music on *Death Certificate*, which is very apparent and necessary. On *AmeriKKKa's Most Wanted*, the Bomb Squad was able to match Cube's delivery and raging energy with tracks just as frenetic and pimped-out. But *Death Certificate* was entirely produced by Cube and longtime partner Sir Jinx. The album is beset by simple funk and R&B loops from the likes of George Clinton's "Atomic Dog" (used a total of eleven times on the album's nineteen songs) or outright samples of the Gap Band and Brick. Though entertaining, the music sounds like a by-product, less important then Ice Cube's screaming tirades and not as pertinent as the subjects and philosophies he espouses. The music neither harms nor enhances *Death Certificate*; ultimately, the album is carried by Ice Cube's sociopolitical call for self-reform and changes in American policy.

Ice-T:
Rhyme Pays (Sire, 1987)
The Iceberg: Freedom of Speech... Just Watch What You Say (Sire, 1989)

by Todd Inoue

Ice-T:
Rhyme Pays

Ice-T:
The Iceberg: Freedom
of Speech... Just Watch
What You Say

A lot of lawyers, politicians, and morality defenders wasted time on Ice-T. His lyrics were a blend of locker room bravado, pulp fiction, and *Manufacturing Consent*. Just like his mentor and namesake Iceberg Slim, Ice-T both glorified and vilified shady street characters and magnified a lifestyle that was hidden to most. And he did it with a voice characterized by surface grit and baritone, a blend that commanded authority and respect—a trait that Hollywood would later pick up on.

Back in the mid-'80s, Ice-T adhered to hip-hop's party rap line by releasing hey-ho singles like "Dog 'n the Wax" and "The Coldest Rap." He was a West Coast dude emulating his East Coast heroes: Kool Herc, Afrika Bambaataa, Melle Mel, and the Cold Crush Brothers. Then, as his South Central neighborhood deteriorated under the crush of Reaganomics and Prop. 13, Ice-T put the plummeting standard of living and the skyrocketing crime rate under the microscope. He portrayed the rapper as a multifaceted and self-assured character, like a gunslinger from a Sergio Leone movie, an image full of contradictions and temptations. He called out crooked cops, yet pimped ho's. He warned against the trap of mental slavery and drugs, but bragged about smacking down bitches and billy badasses.

He spent time working on his degree in street psychology and in 1987, he released his doctoral thesis, *Rhyme Pays*. It sealed Ice-T's reputation as a hard-core rap pioneer, the Calvin Klein of gangsta couture. *Rhyme Pays* contains many of the blueprints that N.W.A., Snoop Dogg, and Master P would later use to make their mint. On some tracks, like "6 'n the Mornin'" and "Somebody Gotta Do It (Pimpin' Ain't Easy!!!)," Ice raps with a frankness and cold detachment. He also conveys the frustrations of the street, especially on "Squeeze the Trigger" and "Pain." Reality rap also meant giving in to carnal desires and Ice busted as many nuts as caps on "Sex" and "I Love Ladies."

The SP-12 was the production weapon of choice, popping off a rapid-fire succession of staccato beats over pre-sample clearance hooks. He pushed rap and rock closer together on the title track, which uses a generous lift from Black Sabbath's "War Pigs." It was a move that capitalized on Run-D.M.C. and Aerosmith's "Walk This Way," but tapped into the aggressive and rebellious nature of heavy metal. Ice would later explore metallurgy in-depth with his thrash group Body Count and a collaboration with Slayer on a cover of Exploited's "War."

"6'n the Mornin'" is *Rhyme Pays*'s magnum opus, as seminal to LA's gangsta rap evolution as Schoolly D's "PSK" was to Philly's. It plays like a condensed version of an inner-city *Sopranos*, covering seven years in the life of a "self-made mobster of the city streets / Remotely controlled by hard hip-hop beats." He dodges the battering ram, shoots dice, beats down punks and bitches, gets arrested, shanks a sucker in the eye, returns to the street, and gets busy in myriad ways. He ends with a trip to New York and then gunshot blasts are heard. The listener wonders what comes next; "But it was 6 'n the morning / We didn't wake up to ask."

Over the next couple of albums, Ice would test his role as the LA streets' most reliable documentarian before and after N.W.A.'s *Straight Outta Compton* (released in 1988) upgraded him from foot soldier to senior correspondent. This era brought forth another gangsta primer, *Power,* and the poignant, bone-chilling first-person narrative called "Colors."

Though 1991's *OG (Original Gangster)* is considered Ice-T's creative high point, he must be praised for going against the grain under extremely hostile circumstances. By the time *The Iceberg: Freedom of Speech … Just Watch What You Say* was released in 1989, Ice-T was at the center of controversy from censors, cops, and up-and-coming rappers (hence the album cover's triple gun penetration artwork). He responds with some of his most acerbic, divisive, and strongest material. He volleys back at his objectors with a full clip: "Peel Their Caps Back" is an inside look at a drive-by shooting; on "The Iceberg," he uses a flashlight as a sex toy.

But it wasn't all cheap thrills. Ice questioned authority with verve. "Lethal Weapon" calls out those who equate his music with depraved violence and gore. "Freedom of Speech" sums up his year defending first amendment rights. "This One's for Me" assails the government, drug addicts, rappers, and commercial radio for selling themselves out. The album's centerpiece, the single "You Played Yourself," is his most graphic indictment of move-fakers trying to profit from chaos. This frankness made him an elder statesman, many miles in front of the guns-blazing stereotype he ushered in. Ice was light-years ahead, fearless in his beliefs. Any other rapper dabbling in homicidal role play wouldn't have had the intelligence or balls to put out a "This One's for Me" or "You Played Yourself" without fear of accusations, blackballing, or reprisals.

He might be known more for his acting than rapping these days, but Ice maintains iconic status. He still releases the occasional album—just to keep his game out there. Other rappers hungry for Hollywood would try to bury a comparably sordid past, but Ice clearly revels in his reputation as street spokesman and gangsta rap godfather. It's served him well; he went on to play many an undercover cop on the big and small screens.

It's a testament to Ice-T's storytelling ability that Charlton Heston—Moses himself—was so enraged by one of the rapper's songs that he performed Ice-T/Body Count karaoke, a cappella, at a Time Warner stockholders meeting. Now that is the coldest rap if there ever was one.

Jay-Z:

Reasonable Doubt (Roc-A-Fella, 1996)
Vol. 3… Life and Times of S. Carter (Roc-A-Fella/Def Jam, 1999)
The Blueprint (Roc-A-Fella/Def Jam, 2001)

by Elizabeth Mendez Berry

Jay-Z:
Reasonable Doubt

Jay-Z:
Vol. 3… Life and Times
of S. Carter

Jay-Z:
The Blueprint

Che Guevara has had an interesting decade. Since his image became part of Rage Against the Machine's logo twenty-five years after his death, popular music has given the Argentine communist more exposure among impressionable youths than his armed struggle ever did. And Rage was just the beginning. At the June 20, 2002, New York party in honor of Andre Harrell's latest protégé Thicke, Jay-Z sported a white T emblazoned with Che's visage—perhaps a case of game recognizing game, but that night it could've been either a tribute or a diss. A diamond-encrusted Roc-a-Fella pendant hung around Jay-Z's neck, and as he moved among a bevy of models, it banged against Guevara's forehead with every step.

The image is audacious but unsurprising. Jay-Z dominates hip-hop, and he's even smacking Latin America's most famous revolutionary upside the head with his philosophy: Can't knock the hustle. Would Che roll over in his grave if he knew that one of capitalism's most devout spokespeople was accessorizing his image with bling that probably cost children in Sierra Leone a few limbs? Probably. But he might also be captivated by Jay's ability to make superficiality seductive. Either way, Che would have to listen up. Jay-Z has ghetto blocks hanging on his every word, the types of impoverished communities that Guevara and pal Fidel Castro tried to liberate through revolution in Cuba.

There's been much debate about Shawn Carter's street career, the personal mythology that has added kilos of weight to Jay-Z-the-rapper's sordid tales. But regardless of Carter's actual criminal exploits, Jay-Z raps like a kingpin: he's articulate, ruthless, in control. While most young MCs are hungry, on his debut, 1996's *Reasonable Doubt*, Jay sounds sated. From Grey Poupon to Dom Perignon, his trademark top-tier tastes are already in evidence here. The (do) rags to riches story that rappers tell after they go platinum was his before he sold his first record. On "Dead Presidents II" he claims, "I dabbled in crazy weight / Without rap, I was crazy straight / Partner, I'm still spending money from eighty-eight."

Both an apologia for his lifestyle and a defiant defense of it, *Doubt* is interesting because it isn't a blind celebration of criminality—it's an unflinching, intelligent one. His unapologetic manifesto, "Can't Knock the Hustle," glamorizes its topic, but also alludes to the deeper roots of gangstas' middle-finger mentality: "All us blacks got is sports and entertainment, until we even / Thievin', as long as I'm breathin' / Can't knock the way a nigga eatin'—fuck you even." Is it society's fault that Jay-Z's a hustler? This question resurfaces throughout his career, often invoked as a convenient excuse for his behavior, but sometimes presented with such perceptive socioeconomic analysis that one wishes he'd rap to George W. on his native Marcy Projects' behalf. He certainly knows what's going on there. Whether he cares or not is much less clear.

Jay's not bad meaning bad, he's bad meaning good. Or at least bad meaning morally conflicted. *Doubt*'s "Regrets" documents one of the riveting moments of ambivalence that make his persona intriguing, ending with a poignant dedication to a deceased friend: "I think I'm touched / This whole verse I been talkin' to your spirit, a little too much." The pregnant pause—more than just a comma—between the word "spirit" and "a little too much" betrays a rare waver.

Doubt's solemn musical tone matches the gravity of Jay-Z's words. DJ Premier's melancholy "D'Evils" uses a minor-key piano sample to underscore Jay's nefarious tales. Songs that could easily become brash bragfests, like "Can I Live," are tempered by both Jay-Z's low-key flow and their somber musical tone; in this case, producer DJ Irv (now known as Irv Gotti) uses horns and subtle strings to frame Jay's bittersweet tale of money and mayhem. The second version of the same track lacks that restraint, as Jay's unrepentant boasting is matched by an equally exultant piano-tickled beat by K-Rob.

Reasonable Doubt was written when Shawn-Carter-the-hustler had barely been laid to rest. Recorded in the wake of the huge commercial success of 1998's *Vol. 2 … Hard Knock Life*, 1999's cold-blooded *Vol. 3 … Life and Times of S. Carter* showcases Jay-Z at his most menacing. The gangsta may have retired, but for Jay, the drug-related metaphors will last forever. Acutely aware of the jealousy he's attracting, on "Come and Get Me" he snarls, "It's only fair that I warn you, rap's my new hustle / I'm treatin' it like the corner." On *Vol. 3* he seems bent on confirming what the December 1, 1999, stabbing of Lance "Un" Rivera (which occurred four weeks prior to *Vol. 3*'s release; Jay initially maintained his innocence regarding the incident before pleading guilty almost two years later) suggested: that his Billboard-bullying mobster persona represents a clear and present danger. On the bonus track "Jigga My Nigga" he raps, "I don't give a fuck if I sold one or one million / But I think you should / 'Cause if I only sold one, then out comes the hood / All black in the club, the outcome ain't good."

But though he spends much of *Vol. 3* intimidating potential victims and haters, Jay also illuminates the emotional life of a gangster. "There's Been a Murder," a vignette in which Jay-Z gets murdered by Shawn-Carter-the-hustler, is a dynamic duet. As Carter he raps: "I held roundtable meetings so we could go on and discuss / not only money but all the emotions goin' through us / Why we don't cry when niggas die, that's how the street raised him / Look in the air, say a prayer hopin' God forgave him / Cop liquor, twist it, tap it twice, pour it to the pavement." Jay-Z humanizes the hustler, revealing the shiver behind the swagger.

Vol. 3 is rich with captivating stories and intermittently great production, notably Timbaland's sparsely brilliant contributions, "It's Hot" and "Come and Get Me." But fame has begun to mess with the usually clear-minded rapper's head. On "Dope Man," a song in which Jay-Z goes on trial for selling drugs (a metaphor for his music), he calls himself "The soul of Mumia in this modern-day time." I don't think so. *Vol. 3* is also marred by collaborations with the likes of Mariah Carey.

After years of walking the line between pop and pap, in 2001 Jay-Z released *The Blueprint*, an unfettered portrait of the hustler in his prime consistent enough to be called *Reasonable Doubt*'s sequel. Jay-Z's life may be filled with private jets, personal chefs, and high-thread-count linens, but don't let anyone accuse him of getting soft in the lap of luxury. The beats are hard, the rhymes are harder, and it's still all about cold hard cash. On the song "U Don't Know" he raps, "Could make 40 off a brick but one rhyme could beat that."

The Blueprint finds the rapper on top of the world and here, he takes the time to enjoy the scenery. Jay-Z skewers his inferiors with laid-back brutality (on "Takeover"), offers love to friends and family (on the title track). And after years of likeable and not-so-likeable lechery (with lines like "The only time you love 'em is when your dick's hard" from *Doubt*'s "Cashmere Thoughts"), Jay-Z allows himself a rare moment of romantic vulnerability on "Song Cry." It's difficult to tell whether he's just throwing his female fans a bone (pun intended) after years of casual misogyny or if this is a genuine moment of introspection from the self-professed groupie connoisseur. Either way, it's earned him love from the ladies.

Jay-Z is convincing. When he raps "I'm representin' for the seat where Rosa Parks sat / Where Malcolm X was shot, where Martin Luther was popped" on *Blueprint*'s "The Ruler's Back," you almost believe him. When he rocks his Guevara shirt and a do-rag, squint and you see a revolutionary. But open your eyes to the platinum chain around his neck: Jay-Z is a hustler. It may be that he recognizes the sex-appeal-by-association of guerrilla garb. Or perhaps in the process of polishing his game till it gleams, it's begun to blind him. Asked why he wore Che's likeness on *Unplugged*, Jay-Z responded that he considers himself a revolutionary like Guevara because he's a self-made black millionaire in a racist society. But he misses the point that for Che, one more millionaire is no reason to celebrate. Guevara abandoned a cushy career in medicine to pursue his lifelong goal, the creation of an egalitarian society uncorrupted by decadence or deprivation, whereas Jay corrupted his community by selling street medication. Later, Che left the relative comfort of celebrity in communist Cuba to stir up revolution throughout Latin America, while Jay ditched dope-dealing for the relative comfort of Big Pimpin' rap. Che died trying to change the world. Jay lives large in the new world order. But even if you can knock Jay-Z's logic, you can't knock the hustle.

Jungle Brothers:
Straight Out the Jungle (Idler, 1988)
Done by the Forces of Nature (Warner Bros., 1989)

De La Soul:
3 Feet High and Rising (Tommy Boy, 1989)
De La Soul Is Dead (Tommy Boy, 1991)
Buhloone Mindstate (Tommy Boy, 1993)

A Tribe Called Quest:
People's Instinctive Travels
and the Paths of Rhythm (Jive, 1990)
The Low End Theory (Jive, 1991)
Midnight Marauders (Jive, 1993)

by Joseph Patel

There's a great temptation to look back on the Native Tongues with blinding sentimentality. Hip-hop has aged enough for there to be an actual bygone era for purists to revere, and there's nothing better than nostalgia for buffing the rough edges and airbrushing the blemishes in order to create grand metaphor. But the bias is not without justification. The union of the Jungle Brothers, De La Soul, and A Tribe Called Quest was not just the conjoining of like-minded artists who broadened the range and tenor of hip-hop with their colorful look and language. The Native Tongues were the manifestation of idealism itself: young intellectuals and artists feeling out the world with a proud, knowing, and youthful sense of self and community. While they invoked a new rap bohemia by linking their music to the world around them, they more importantly created an environment within hip-hop and its culture that could embrace such alternative views. That contribution perpetuates

Jungle Brothers:
Straight Out the Jungle

Jungle Brothers:
Done by the Forces
of Nature

the Native Tongues legacy and will continue to do so—even when its members have long since stopped rapping.

The Native Tongues began with the Jungle Brothers: rappers Afrika Baby Bam and Mike G, and DJ Sammy B. From the first moments of their debut album, *Straight Out the Jungle*, the group emerged as the blackest of black. The sticky mix of James Brown, Manu Dibango, and Mandrill samples that forms the opening title track traces the lineage between the group's vivid funk and the diaspora of their heritage. Moreover, through lyrics, imagery, and inference, they use *Jungle* and its follow-up, *Done by the Forces of Nature*, to create an urban tribalism symbolizing the black experience in white America. That mentality was part of a revived Afrocentricism, which was burgeoning in the streets and migrating to the college campuses and the suburbs. Also developing at the time were the concepts of community, and with knock-wood beaded necklaces enhancing their message, songs like "Black Is Black" and "Tribe Vibes" were saying, "We're all in this together."

The JBs were unapologetically *African*-American, and their inclusive ideals were a reaction to the quixotic isolationism that was the socioeconomic pathology of the Reagan/Bush '80s. The community-building at the core of Afrocentricism was central to the Native Tongues. These three artists developed their own strong individual identities, but still came together as a collective sans ego or hierarchy (initially, at least). They called themselves a family or a tribe on songs like De La Soul's "Buddy" (and on its classic, jubilant remix) and the Jungle Brothers' "Doin' Our Own Dang." And an entire generation of hard-luck to middle-class urban youth who were looking for real-world inspiration found it. The Native Tongues might not have been the impetus toward a growing black esteem, but by being the soundtrack and medium for the movement's messages, they certainly provided momentum.

There was no "pop" submerged in either of the Jungle Brothers' first two albums. Both were all dirty funk, especially the debut, which stripped away the drums so that its rhythms were elegantly muscled, and chunky soul and funk samples were layered in a near cubist array. "Jimbrowski" is rightfully remembered for its colorful wordplay and euphemism, but also for its beefy yet animated sonic pastiche. The echoing drum-machine hits and the ghostly reverb of Red Alert's laugh and DJ call, "Here we go," are quintessential identifiers for hip-hop in the late '80s. As for the MCs, Baby Bam's congested flow gave him the timbered tone of a pious pitchman, and Mike G was almost indiscernibly the same. Both rapped in measured, speakeasy cadences that allowed their earnestness to cut through the clutter of "braggin' and boastin'" that defined hip-hop at the time. The one song that transcended the popularity of the album itself was "I'll House You," which was a play on both hip-hop slang and the up-tempo dance floor beats of house music, the genre that was dominating New York clubs in the late '80s. It wasn't meant to be ironic—beats is beats. The Jungle Brothers saw house as part of hip-hop's musicology, but nobody else did.

Done by the Forces of Nature played more like a complete work than the collection of singles its predecessor seemed to be. As an Afrocentric manifesto it was a tour de force, celebrating the Native Tongues themes of family, unity, heritage, and independence while sublimating them into more melodic context. And some songs unraveled at a much faster pace, like the first two frenetic cuts, "Beyond This World" and "Feelin' Alright." The array of African chants and chaw-jawed blues verses from Baby Bam and Mike G, the honey-suckled guitar licks, and the scat singing evoked a time-warped Broadway music revue of Afrocentricity. But then this was the Jungle Brothers' role: being the bricklayers for a new black mentality.

Up until De La Soul released their debut album, *3 Feet High and Rising*, and its monster single, "Me Myself and I," hip-hop had only ever come from the hardened streets of the inner city; in New York that meant the Bronx, Queens, Brooklyn, or Harlem. Posdnous (aka Plug One), Trugoy (aka Dove, aka Plug Two), and Maseo (aka PA Mase, aka Plug Three) were from Long Island—the 'Burbs. What their music constituted metaphorically could now be understood literally (i.e., they came from left field) and their success proved that hip-hop wasn't just about inner-city plight, but was a full-fledged means for communication. De La's emergence from this unwitting locale made it possible for cities like Atlanta to eventually spawn their own hip-hop communities. It also signified that hip-hop had matriculated toward the middle class.

3 Feet High and Rising is one of the great achievements in hip-hop music for one specific reason: language. These teenagers created a world rich in slang, euphemism, imagery, and metaphor that was just as fluorescent as the Day-Glo pink and yellow ornamenting the album's cover. De La Soul told stories in code, juggled their syntax, took on multiple identities, and crafted so many layers of intricate and illusory lyrical "imagineering" that each listen revealed something you had never understood before. What was "Buddy" and who was "Jenifa" and what were the "Potholes in My Lawn"? Deciphering even just a fraction of what De La Soul encrypted was to gain entry into a bohemian Wonderland. This was the "D.A.I.S.Y. Age" and they were "Delacratic." They could—and would—do anything.

The sonic language authored by producer, erstwhile Stetsasonic DJ, and unofficial fourth member Prince Paul was just as brilliant. His collagist splurges and schizophrenic arrangements gave depth to the album (matching the rappers' allusion and illusion note for note) and revolutionized how sampling was done. For his mining of music beyond the obvious (funk, James Brown, Parliament/Funkadelic) and into the arcane ('60s pop, lounge, soft rock) Prince Paul is the patron saint for beat-diggers everywhere. He unassumingly declared that any piece of music could be cribbed, looped, layered, and otherwise manipulated into its own narrative. (Maybe he was too good; faced with something they clearly didn't understand and with no framework in place to help them digest his technological ethos, the courts held steadfast in their conservatism, claiming any sampling was a fatal breach of intellectual property laws. Those laws still hold today even though taken as a whole, *3 Feet High* is the most compelling piece of evidence in the argument for hip-hop as original postmodern expression.)

Prince Paul also understood the essence of an "album" as a conceptual piece of work like no artist before him. Together with the De La triumvirate, he will be infamously remembered for using the hip-hop skit to frame an album (in *3 Feet's* case, the album is situated in the context of an absurd game show). This tool gains its infamy from being overdone for a decade-plus. Confirming Prince Paul's peculiar grasp on reality—and to prove a point about the skit's absurdity—he made an entire album, *Psychoanalysis*, composed of nothing but skits.

While *3 Feet High and Rising* could be considered the group's best work, the trio's artistry and genius is maybe even better illustrated by the follow-up album, *De La Soul Is Dead*. De La Soul's self-conscious "suicide" was a clever way to kill off the decorative underpinnings they felt limited their expression (e.g., being labeled "hippies" for their too-bohemian vibe) without sacrificing the substance of their craft. They mocked their popularity on the album's skits—which featured a schoolyard bully trying to beat up a kid for his De

La Soul tape—and balanced the ego necessary for compelling hip-hop with a healthy and heretofore absent sense of self-deprecation.

Thanks again to Prince Paul, *De La Soul Is Dead* was just as intricately stitched as its predecessor, though it posed as dark comedy. The sentiment was captured in the unforgettable image of a fallen pot of daisies, which proclaimed that the D.A.I.S.Y. Age, the time of vibrant innocence that marked *3 Feet High and Rising*, was nevermore. Posdnous rhymed poignantly about his brother falling victim to crack ("My Brother's a Basehead"), and he and Trugoy told an even darker tale of incest and revenge ("Millie Pulled a Pistol on Santa"). "Ring Ring Ring (Ha Ha Hey)" even expressed the group's manic frustration with fame. But playfulness still abounded on the album; witness the Native Tongues disco fever of "A Roller Skating Jam Named 'Saturdays'" and the rhyming dozens of "Bitties in the BK Lounge." *De La Soul Is Dead* was the perfect antithesis to their debut: it managed to be both the same as and different from *3 Feet High and Rising*.

If De La Soul made you feel like you were in another world, A Tribe Called Quest were speaking the language of the here and now. It was A Tribe Called Quest— Q-Tip, Phife, and Ali Shaheed Muhammad—who bridged the Native Tongues, since it was through Q-Tip that the other two groups met. Tribe was a stylistic median as well, taking the Jungle Brothers' communal inspiration and matching it with De La Soul's imaginative bohemianism. The individual parts of the group were nothing spectacular: Q-Tip rapped like he had the flu, Phife was the penultimate hype man, and Ali Shaheed Muhammad would never be confused with DJ Premier. Yet together in a studio, these three seemingly spare parts emitted transcendent, magical chemistry, as is evident on their debut, *People's Instinctive Travels and the Paths of Rhythm*.

A Tribe Called Quest understood the essence of young urban people and expressed themselves as sage peers who empathized with expectations, frustrations, elation, and pain. Q-Tip, the lustful poet, rapped about real life while Phife played

De La Soul:
3 Feet High and Rising

De La Soul:
De La Soul Is Dead

De La Soul:
Buhloone Mindstate

A Tribe Called Quest:
People's Instinctive
Travels and the Paths
of Rhythm

A Tribe Called Quest:
The Low End Theory

A Tribe Called Quest:
Midnight Marauders

his devilish counterpart and Ali Shaheed cued up a soundtrack of De La–like psychedelic soul and pop (sampling everything from the Beatles to Lou Reed to rare groove). "Footprints" is a heartfelt monologue that articulates freedom and the desire to do something great, while "Luck of Lucien" and "I Left My Wallet in El Segundo" are classic storytelling episodes. This record was almost more bohemian than either the Jungle Brothers or De La Soul, but somehow the listener never had to suspend their belief to follow along.

Still, A Tribe Called Quest initially seemed unlikely candidates for becoming the most popular group in the Native Tongues. But that's exactly what they would become when they released their second album, *The Low End Theory*. If ever an album understood the direction in which music was heading, it is this classic work. Short, eloquent, and mature, *The Low End Theory* was a consummate link between generations, taking the essence of jazz and the essence of hip-hop and showing they originated from the same black center. Others sampled jazz or used jazz instruments, but that was veneering. Tribe incorporated jazz's spirit into their being and came up with gems like "Excursion," which explained the generational link; "Verses from the Abstract," which sampled Grant Green's down-tempo rhythms; and "Check the Rhime," which turned into a summer anthem in 1991. The video for the latter showed Tribe rapping on a rooftop in front of their Queens people, but you could've put folks from any city there; Tribe connected to their broader audience in ways other groups didn't know how to. "I love my young nation," Q-Tip says on "Scenario" —and it loved him back.

By 1991, it was clear that the Native Tongues were tapping into the consciousness of young people. They became synonymous with anything substantive, emotionally charged, or communal—and just about everyone wanted to be down. Monie Love and Queen Latifah were already honorary members (Latifah's "Mama Gave Birth to the Soul Children" with De La Soul was her primary Native Tongues collaboration). If any other group were to be officially indoctrinated into the Native Tongues it would be Black Sheep, who debuted that same year with *A Wolf in Sheep's Clothing*. While *Wolf* embodied the same elements as the other three members' music, it spun them with a sarcastic consciousness and Dres's devastating wit. And there were other groups being described as Native Tongues–*like* for their embrace of family, poetry, sampling, or messages: KMD, Brand Nubian, Leaders of the New School, and on the West Coast a short time later, Souls of Mischief, Pharcyde, and Freestyle Fellowship. With two albums each under their belts, the Native Tongues seemed to have led the young hip-hop nation to the Promised Land of ideals and ever after.

But it was too good to be true. The same forces that were inspiring others to be down with the Native Tongues would ultimately bury the group under affiliation. Such is the problem with too-democratic environments; some self-selection is needed to maintain the founding ideals. Once third-generation Chi Ali started to use his affiliation as a marketing tool, the core trio realized things weren't the same. If they were speaking to each other, that is. While Tribe and De La were touring the country together, the Jungle Brothers were nowhere to be found.

The third album released by each group would be telling. The Jungle Brothers' freakfest *J. Beez Wit the Remedy* was their first for a major label (Warner Bros.), but its dissonant beats and dystopian rhymes reflected the isolation the group had imposed on itself from the rest of the Native Tongues "family." It is almost unlistenable, though the Q-Tip remix of "On the Road" hinted at what could have been for Native Tongues post-1992. Drugs and discontentment were said to be the culprits behind *J. Beez*, but the weak release could simply have been a product of the group's desire to carve out their own identity after the movement they helped to initiate failed to provide them with creative sustenance.

De La Soul's *Buhloone Mindstate* was the group's clean break from the duality of their first two albums: it was shorter, it cut back on the skits, and it attempted to move out from under the shadow of Prince Paul. The shift was understandable; De La Soul had never wanted to be typecast, nor were they content to let someone else guide their careers when they had aspirations of their own. *Buhloone Mindstate* was its own kaleidoscopic indulgence, but unlike *J. Beez*, it had reflective (and distiguishable) rhymes that nudged up against sentiment and hinted that the group was getting older. Always quotable, Posdnous threw out one of his best lines, a defiant boast, on "In the Woods": "Fuck being hard, Posdnous is complicated." But he would also say, "That native shit is done so the stickabush is coming," which would hint at the demise of the Native Tongues union. He explained further on "I Am I Be," a touching song of self-reflection that symbolized the vulnerability De La Soul revealed, but hip-hop was generally afraid of: "Or some tongues who lied / and said, 'We'll be natives to the end' / Nowadays we don't even speak / I guess we got our own life to live / Or is it because we want our own kingdom to rule?" For someone like Posdnous, who rarely wasted a word in his rhymes and encouraged others to decipher them, this was a damning statement on the future of the Native Tongues.

While the Jungle Brothers were stretching the union one way, Tribe was stretching the seams in another direction. Their third album, *Midnight Marauders*, would be their masterwork. It's hard to believe they could top *The Low End Theory*, but A Tribe Called Quest did so. Their new crew extended beyond the Native Tongues and included all of hip-hop—as shown by the faces depicted on the album's front and back covers—and Tribe was quickly becoming the one group who could negotiate both underground respect and aboveground fame. *Midnight Marauders* worked all the elements that constituted Tribe previously to utter perfection: storytelling; anthemic singles; sexually charged rhymes; innovative production; and an exploration of life experiences, emotion, sentiment, history, and heritage. As hip-hop began to change and stratify and develop into generations and geographies, *Midnight Marauders* could have been the last record that every single hip-hopper —whether from Queensbridge or Queensland, whether gangsta or wannabe poet —had in their collection.

And that is the history etched by the Native Tongues. Public Enemy, Boogie Down Productions, and X-Clan may have provided the most bombast in reigniting the passion for black pride with their sonic calls to arms and their megaphone grandstanding. But the Native Tongues held a more potent social platform rooted not in politics, but in identity: pride, self-awareness, and the ability and confidence to function individually and as a family. Each album that the group delivered in their time was a manifesto of freedom and unity, burned forever into the hip-hop consciousness. And whether the year is 1989 or 2089, their ideas will live on—even if they themselves do not. In light of this achievement they deserve to be remembered fondly and with a little naïveté. That innocence makes their existence that much more inspiring.

Juvenile: 400 Degreez (Uptown/Universal, 1998)

by Tony Green

B.G.: Chopper City in the Ghetto (Uptown/Universal, 1999)

Juvenile:
400 Degreez

B.G.:
Chopper City in
the Ghetto

By 2002—the mid part of 2001, actually—rap's "entertainment for its own sake" era was terminal. Maybe not in terms of its presence on the charts—the lightweight but successful popmeisters (Mr. Cheeks), the could-be-interesting-but-why-bothers (Ja Rule), and the talented but content-bereft (Ludacris) were still finding sales success—but there was a definite shift in sensibilities among the core, grassroots hip-hop audience.

Even before the much publicized Coup/World Trade Center flap, the hip-hop community, as well as a growing number of artists, were leaning toward (to paraphrase dead prez) Huey P. rather than Master P. Like a club rat reaching for a glass of orange juice and B vitamins after a Cristal binge, hip-hop's listening public started to seek entertainment with less fluffy nutritional values. By the time Russell Simmons organized a mini musicfest protesting education budget cuts in the New York City School System, "raptivism" had become enough of a buzzword to make it into the *Washington Post*, and "bling bling" was a term not even worth dissing anymore.

So what to make of the Big Tymers' *Hood Rich*, which debuted at number one on the pop charts in the early summer of 2002? Arguably the most hedonistic hip-hop crew ever, Cash Money had the southern rap game on lock from 1998–2000 before hitting a sales dry spell. Mannie Fresh and Baby were outrageous even by the Cristal-and-designer-jewelry standards of the '90s. Cash Money seemed even more unreconstructed when read against the mood that greeted their return; while hip-hop was asserting its sociopolitical muscle, they were still extolling the virtues of living high and getting paid and laid. "Can't pay my rent / 'cause all my money's spent" is not the lyrical stuff nations are built on.

But if there was one thing the mid- to late '90s taught us, it was that hip-hop's geniuses were often the people who made the sounds, not the words. A hip-hop audience entranced by Biggie's peerless wordplay could be just as engaged by his less talented Bad Boy cohorts (Ma$e, Puffy), provided that the tracks were hittin'. Along the same lines, Master P. proved that southern heads who worshiped Tupac and West Coast funk would buy knockoff product as long as it got a party started. It was all about the head-nod, baby; tracks by producers like Timbaland and Swizz Beats were often more memorable than the raps on top of them. Cash Money's reappearance on the charts, then, simply reminded people that sometimes all you need is a drummer (digital or otherwise) for people who more often than not only need a beat.

Like fellow Louisianian P., Cash Money was a New Orleans indie made good, landing a thirty-million-dollar deal with Universal in 1997. Also like their hometown forerunner, they cranked out glossy, ghettocentric product (complete with garishly ghetto-fab Pen-n-Pixel–designed covers) that created its own reason for existing.

Lyrically, the Cash Money clique never left the confines of the Magnolia projects. Tunes like Lil' Wayne's "Tha Block Is Hot," "#1 Stunna," and "Back That Azz Up" were about nothing more than life on the grind. Flossing in luxury cars with the price sticker still on them, sipping Cristal through platinum-plated grills, hitting fat project asses from the back, balling on the block—this was life for the Cash Money brothas. Nihilistic? Sure. But the music made the ride more than worth it.

Unlike P.'s often derivative tracks, CM's production—handled almost exclusively by board wizard Mannie Fresh—was an innovative, relentless amalgam of old-school electro, southern funk, and the New Orleans homegrown sound, "Bounce" music.

The crew's showcase artist, Juvenile (Terius Gray), was a longtime New Orleans underground star; his "Bounce for the Juvenile" was the cut that gave bounce music its name. Juvenile's *400 Degreez* caught heads sleeping big-time, on a number of levels. First there was the raw beatology of tunes like the Tito Puente–influenced banger "Follow Me Now." Mannie Fresh, who once made a beat out of a mayonnaise jar, was in his lo-fi glory, melding Mantronix-influenced rhythms with a slip-sliding combination of programmed and live instrumentation. Then there was the street-art vérité of the accompanying video, shot in and around his home projects.

Juvie's lyrics were what really got people open, though. Rather, the *sound* of his lyrics. The album's hit single, "Ha" ("huh" or "youknowhatimsayin" in Magnoliaspeak) dropped in the summer of '98 like the left hook you never saw coming. Juvie's Crescent City slanguage flowed over bar lines:

"That's you in the big body Benz, ha / That's you who can't keep an old lady / 'cause you keep fuckin' her friends, ha." And on the other standout track, "Ghetto Children," Juvie demonstrates his mastery of the singsongy flow that was a Cash Money trademark.

B.G. (Baby Gangsta), on the other hand, was the darker side to the Cash Money party. Folks like Juve and the Big Tymers extolled the virtues of living high on the hog while B.G. dwelled in the murky world where the deeds that made all the flossing possible got done. Juvenile once said that "you get two niggas together in a room in New Orleans, and five minutes later there will be some shootin' goin' on." This is the city B.G. breaks down on tunes like "Hard Times," "Real Niggaz," and "Bout My Paper." Despite cuts like the buzzword-spawning "Bling Bling," the pussy-chasing "Dog Ass," and over-the-top interludes by the Big Tymers, *Chopper City* was the most street-fatalistic album to come out of the Cash Money stable. His woozily menacing turn on "Trigga Play" (B.G. struggled with heroin addiction throughout his Cash Money tenure) evoked memories of "Deep Cover"-era Snoop ("I'm bout that trigga play nigga / ... / I come thru your area to bury you"). And the slasher-flick backing on the equally threatening "Thug'n" heralded Mannie Fresh's late '90s love affair with synthesized texture.

Though the crew produced plenty of destructive grooves later in their late '90s reign (say, around 1999–2000), it's hard to argue with the raw potency of the first wave of records produced under their deal with Universal. It's ironic that two of the best albums from this era—Juvenile's *400 Degreez* and B.G.'s *Chopper City in the Ghetto*—were put out by artists who, by the time of Cash Money's resurrection, had broken from the label, citing differences over money and royalties. But then again, that's the way it's always been in New Orleans, a town fraught with rivalry and violent internecine feuds (the story of Cash Money's first independent-era success, UNLV, is a book in and of itself). As this is being written, Cash Money is rolling with a new set of artists—and even a second producer (Jazzy Pha)—back on the grind, looking forward to the day when, for even the briefest moment, it'll all be gravy, baby.

LL Cool J:
Radio (Def Jam, 1985)
Mama Said Knock You Out (Def Jam, 1990)

by Lefty Banks

LL Cool J:
Radio

LL Cool J:
Mama Said Knock
You Out

For all his accolades, one of LL Cool J's most dubious accomplishments is having invented the worst album title in hip-hop history: *G.O.A.T.* (2000). It's one thing to call yourself the Greatest of All Time. It's quite another to pen an acronym that conjures up a self-image replete with long shaggy hair and horns. On the other hand, if LL wants to call himself the Greatest of All Time (in whatever form), he's more or less welcome to. A hip-hop veteran who's been in the game since age thirteen, LL has outlasted (and outsold) practically every mentor, peer, and protégé he's ever had.

Though he waited until his second album to use the title *Bigger and Deffer*, the sentiment could have just as easily applied to his seminal debut, *Radio* (1985). In essence, LL did everything bigger than what had come before him, fashioning himself—as a teen, no less—into a larger-than-life icon that defined the modern MC. He wasn't the first braggadocio rapper by any means, and stylistically he owed obvious debts to both Def Jam labelmate T La Rock and fellow Queens rockers Run-D.M.C., but even their considerable bravado paled in comparison.

On 1985's *Radio*, LL Cool J emerges as hip-hop's first rock superstar: a golden god of black masculinity, exuding presence and swagger. Though rap music had already established itself as the realm of testosterone-powered posturing, LL's utter self-confidence and omnipotent attitude fashioned a new ideal that towered over his predecessors. When he spits "LL Cool J is hard as hell" on "Rock the Bells," there's no way to deny or even question the sheer *rightness* of the statement. There is no "if" to be debated: LL *is* hard as hell.

We take it for granted now that such bluster is just a normal part of the MC routine, but LL was armed with more than ambitious rhetoric to bolster his claims. At the time, you got the idea that he knew no one could fuck with him. Every verse was a taunt, every line a put-down (whether literal or implied), and he was so self-assured that it was hard not to buy into his self-created supremacy. But more than just his boasting acumen, LL shows innovative finesse with his compact rhyme scheme and a flow that accents each syllable perfectly. Check how the then sixteen-year-old already lays claim to the G.O.A.T. title with a verse from "You'll Rock" that demonstrates his multifaceted angles of attack: "I'll dust a rapper off if I require practice / Vocal cords so rough that I can eat cactus / Choreographer of rhymes, best of all times / Composition technician with the b-boy's mind."

On *Radio* LL also exudes the charisma that makes Ladies Love Cool James; he's a b-boy Casanova with a grown man's strut. Songs like "I Want You" and "I Can Give You More" build on Spoonie Gee's love raps, but LL's unflappable self-confidence, combined with a seductive baritone, is another leap ahead of his forebears. Unlike the unsalvageable syrupiness of his later ballad smash "I Need Love," his bedroom rhymes on *Radio* sound like slightly softer variations on "I Can't Live Without My Radio" and "I Need a Beat"—his cocksure masculinity is manifest whether he's trying to charm pants down or simply knock them off.

Behind all this is Rick Rubin's minimalist production, a sparse but powerful mesh of thunderous drum machine programming, crashing cymbals, jagged guitar stabs, and slicing cuts by DJ Cut Creator. Like the Beastie Boys' *Licensed to Ill* or

Run-D.M.C.'s *Raising Hell*, both of which followed in 1996, *Radio* features Rubin finding an ideal mesh between rock's turn-it-to-11 sound wall and hip-hop's funkadelic polyrhythms. Mantronix might still be the better-respected drum programmers, but you'd be a fool not to give Rubin his due here. His spiraling, splattering percussive assaults fit LL's own relentless rhyme attack perfectly, from the bombastic slam of "Rock the Bells" to the chaotic clash of rhythms on "You Can't Dance" to the deceptively light piano tinkles and shuffling drums on "I Can Give You More."

For all of *Radio*'s strengths, LL's next two albums couldn't capitalize on the brashness of his debut. *Bigger and Deffer* (1987) was a respectable follow-up, but by 1989's *Walking with a Panther*, LL was beginning to verge on irrelevancy, especially in an era where other MCs like Chuck D and Rakim had sprinted ahead of LL in terms of critical acclaim and street credibility. One can argue endlessly over whether or not LL's 1990 *Mama Said Knock You Out* is rightfully a "comeback" album or not—the man himself postures on the title track: "Don't call it a comeback"—but it was a reinvention at the very least.

LL's wisest decision at this point in his career was to hook up with Marley Marl, who was then at the top of his game as hip-hop's foremost trackmaster. Marley's first move was to remix "Jingling Baby," a likeable but lackluster song from *Walking with a Panther* that became dance floor dynamite with Marl's revamp. The initial fit would prove auspicious and Marley ended up producing LL's entire fourth album, *Mama Said Knock You Out.*

As with *Radio*, LL also has a point to prove on *Mama*, but rather than taking over the world, he's now battling to rescue the throne that everybody else had all but assumed he'd lost. On "Cheesy Rat Blues," LL takes a tongue-in-cheek approach to his fallen status by joking, "I go to the park, they wanna baseball-bat me / I go to the mall, they throw my old tapes at me." But with *Mama*, LL storms the street corner, reinventing his champagne-sipping, party boy image into one of a street-stoop sage, whether he's penning a lowrider anthem on "Boomin' System," shouting-out all neighborhood honeys on "Around the Way Girl," or taking a slap at police overseers with the New Jack Swingin' "Illegal Search." His old hunger still manifests with explosive force on tracks like the fast rap "Murdergram," and his verses off the album's title track are as pugnaciously fierce as the boxing imagery in the song's video.

With songs like the surprisingly spiritual "The Power of God" and the humorously risqué "Milky Cereal," *Mama* has lasted as LL's most diverse and complete album, well balanced in its various moods and without any of the wince-inducing corniness of his older material. Even his requisite love ballad, "6 Minutes of Pleasure," sounds thoughtful and reflective despite Marley Marl's quiet storm track. The two (LL and Marley) have a fantastic partnership on the album and from the slow-bumping bass knocker on "The Boomin' System" to the herky-jerky funk snap on "Eat 'Em Up L Chill," Marl finds the right note to sound with LL's own selections of styles.

After proving that he could still take the MC title, LL summarily slid back into irrelevance after *Mama*, releasing a string of commercial hit singles but nary a remotely classic album. Yet, for the one rapper who's survived and thrived in the rap game for almost twenty years now, you can never completely count LL out. Rap's first and lasting shining prince, LL's earned his propers. Or in his own words, he's "been here for years, rocking his peers and putting suckers in fear."

by Zenobia Simmons

MC Lyte: Lyte As a Rock (First Priority, 1988)
Queen Latifah: All Hail the Queen (Tommy Boy, 1989)

MC Lyte:
Lyte As a Rock

Queen Latifah:
All Hail the Queen

One night when I came home so late it was actually early morning, I discovered my sister sitting mesmerized in front of the TV. She was watching a video featuring a short, tough-looking girl in a sweat suit with huge doorknockers rhyming about how hard she was. I had to find out who this tomboy was, kicking some of the most hardcore rhymes I had ever heard from any MC—male or female. I asked my sister, "Who is that?"

"This girl named MC Lyte," she replied.

There were a lot of female MCs before Lyte, but at the time she was the first to define a new voice for women in hip-hop. Lyte proved that a female rap artist could sell records and be different from the usual booty-shaking, feel-good, female MC acting as sexpot or met puppet. Lyte rhymed about dissing her crackhead-ass ex, rocking parties, and battling other MCs. Two of the best songs on *Lyte As a Rock* were "Paper Thin" and "I Cram 2 Understand U." "Paper Thin" was like nothing I had ever heard. Produced by King of Chill (like most of the album), its sharp rim shot, screaming horns, and background chorus of signifying "Ooohs" made it one of those sparse, ear-opening beats only found in early '90s rap. Lyrically, Lyte was at the top of her game, rejecting declarations of love as just "chit chatter" and playing mind games with unsuspecting suitors.

"I Cram 2 Understand U" was a brilliant follow-up to "Paper Thin" for both its storytelling and its originality. Detailing the tragic story of Lyte's teenage heartache because of Sam, she reveals a vulnerable side of her microphone persona and utters her catch phrase "Shut the fuck up!" over a hypnotic 808 beat. There are other note-worthy cuts on the album: "Lyte As a Rock," "MC Lyte Likes Swingin'," and, of course, "10% Diss," one of the all-time greatest diss songs in rap music. Before hip-hop beefs were handled with violence and publicity smear campaigns, MCs handled it the old-fashioned way: with beats and rhymes. Lyte starts off hitting hard with the opening lines, "Hot damn ... ho, here we go again." Lyte destroyed her nemesis, Antoinette, with a lyrical ass-whipping so devastating, it ended the poor girl's career.

In fact, Lyte shut it down so hard with "10% Diss" that no other MC tried to step to her again. There was no one who could compare with Lyte until the following year, 1989. Queen Latifah's debut album, *All Hail the Queen*, was another herstorical milestone that came at a time when rap music was expanding and becoming more sophisticated. Latifah was one of the first artists to benefit from this growth. Her album was dramatically different from the standard rap albums being released by her peers. One of the main sources of this album's brilliance was that Latifah could rhyme as well (and better) than any male MC—and she could sing. She was extremely versatile and *All Hail* reflected a mix of musical exchanges with reggae, R&B, and house with an all-star line up of producers and guest artists that included Monie Love, Daddy-O, De La Soul, Soulshock, Mark the 45 King, KRS-One, Prince Paul, and Louie Vega.

All Hail was an album full of powerful singles. "Dance for Me" (the original version) tapped into hip-hop's upbeat, funky-drummer era, but it was on songs like "Latifah's Law" and "Wrath of My Madness" that she took command, displaying

flashes of her pre-Grammy greatness by throwing her heart and soul into a regal, authoritative delivery. It's telling that on "Mama Gave Birth to the Soul Children," Latifah showed she could hang with De La's existential rhymes and quirky style, but when she hooked up with Stetsasonic's Daddy-O on "The Pros," her dubbed-out tirade against "bad breath biters" tapped directly into the sweet 'n sweaty vibe of an underground reggae club.

But the biggest song on the album, "Ladies First," became Latifah's claim to fame. Trading "righteous rhymes" and tongue twisters with Monie Love, she created one of the earliest feminist hip-hop anthems. Although Apache is listed as the sole author on the album credits, Monie and Latifah's voices breathe everlasting life into the cut.

Bringing things full circle were "Princess of the Posse" and "Inside Out." On the drunken, loopy drums of "Princess," it is evident why she was the first and best choice to bring fame to her Flavor Unit crew: she has the rare ability to give mass commercial appeal to a gritty, underground cut. She chats/sings on the hook, "The princess of the posse me say she a cool girl / She rhyme Brooklyn, the Bronx, USA, the world." Slowing it down, she murders the seductively slow track "Inside Out": "My homeboy said this is the D.A.I.S.Y. Age. / I take it as meaning you got to get crazy paid." Taking shots at shady types trying to infiltrate the Queendom, Latifah's angry delivery seems to channel that simmering rage and frustration only truly poetic MCs are able to capture.

Pioneers in every sense of the word, both women helped carve out a niche for themselves in the phallic-inclined world of hip-hop. Without these albums there would be no Lil' Kim, Foxy Brown, or Lauryn Hill. MC Lyte and Queen Latifah achieved more acclaim and commercial success with later albums, but none of their other efforts came as close to musical perfection as these two stellar debuts.

by Serena Kim

Mobb Deep: The Infamous (Loud, 1995)

Mobb Deep:
The Infamous

If an album could have a climate, Mobb Deep's *The Infamous* would be a windless, drizzling rain. It's the soundtrack of project stairwell beat-downs and troops to the weed spot in the dead of winter. "I keep it real / Packin' steel," begins Prodigy on "Start of Your Ending." He couldn't have known that in the next two years, that credo (which was so faithfully lived by and expounded on by masses of rap fans) would ultimately destroy hip-hop as we once knew it through the deaths of Biggie and Tupac. Nobody criticizes Stephen King for not actually killing people in his spare time. Fantasy, science fiction, murder mysteries—none of these bodies of literature would exist if we expected the authors to actually "keep it real." Yet in those days, it was so important in hip-hop for the archetypal rapper to have lived his lyrics—to be authentic.

Thank God that Prodigy didn't literally live his lyrics. He probably spent more time in a hospital bed battling the real demon of sickle-cell anemia than sticking up bodegas and collecting interest on extortion. But Prodigy was Albert Johnson's alter ego (like Todd Shaw's Too $hort), a persona that allowed him to possess the criminal-minded ruthlessness that wasn't feasible in real life. But he could have that viciousness in art, which didn't make it any less valued or real. Instead of languishing in jail or death, P and Havoc wrote songs that permitted us to live the trife life vicariously.

On "The Infamous Prelude," he informs us that he carries a burner and has done his little bids at the thug-infested Muse and Tunnel nightclubs. Regardless of his small stature, he can hold his own. "If you step to me on a personal level, I don't back down easy, know what I'm saying," he growls. "There's a good chance that you'll get shot, stabbed or knuckled down—one of the three, so don't gamble with your life." With that warning established, Prodigy and Havoc continue to take us on a guided tour of their Queensbridge, a version that exists in the zone between life and death, like the abyss-mal purgatory where Tim Robbins's character was trapped in *Jacob's*

Ladder. Over a fast and haunting beat on "Shook Ones Pt. II," Havoc poses the question, "Am I going to burn in hell for all the things I did?/No time to dwell on that 'cause my brain reacts." Mobb Deep's lyrical modus operandi is to struggle with their sins, paranoia, and the existentialism of the New York court system.

Mobb Deep has a complete and organic vision for their music that transcends the short-term goals of rah-rah lyrics and Tunnel-banging production. They make the songs that articulate this nihilistic vision and the rest falls into place. Rather than perfunctorily filling mandatory song types—the mama song, the party anthem, the posse cut, for example—with mundane album tracks, the duo pushes for less conventional approaches to these templates. The wifey song is actually an ode to addiction, "Drink Away the Pain." Prodigy anthropomorphizes his addiction into a long-term crush over a deceptively dulcet horn lick crafted by Q-Tip—incarnated in this song once as a producer (Abstract) and again as a rhyming label whore. On joints like "Cradle to the Grave," "Right Back at You," and "Start of Your Ending," Havoc's minor-key production is monotone without being monotonous, while perfectly matching the sentiment behind the lyrics. He punctures each cheer-less bassline with a shrill clap that echoes like a sledgehammer ringing out on the chain-gang field.

But when he does dole out a melody, it is as poignant as a rap song can get. Over Norman Conner's "You Are My Starship"—a loop that is truncated to play up its dark and menacing attributes—Prodigy and Havoc trade perspectives from two different sides of the same story. Prodigy plays the role of the man that is set up by a propositioning girl in a faraway ghetto. On his verse, Havoc tells the story of using a girl to set up an outsider. Despite the misogyny and hate that imbue each verse, the pathos of the song subtly acknowledges the tragedy at play.

This unmistakably grim yet poetic aesthetic is the signature of Queensbridge's many talented rappers and producers (think Cormega, Nature, L.E.S., and Nas, not Infamous Mobb or Bars and Hooks). Maybe it's because some of them are the offspring of a generation of Southern black artists and writers that were attracted by the prospect of a safe community with affordable rent and more space to raise their children. It was a dream deferred.

Mos Def & Talib Kweli:

by Hua Hsu

Mos Def & Talib Kweli Are Black Star (Rawkus, 1998)

Mos Def & Talib Kweli:
Mos Def & Talib Kweli
Are Black Star

University of California at Berkeley, Fall 1998: The world was ready to change. In California, a voter initiative had just stricken affirmative action the year before and as bright-eyed young student-activists sensing a change in the political currents, we were digging in for the struggle to preserve all the things we (still) believed in: ethnic studies, prison reform, bilingual education, etc. We were going to tear this mothersucker down and make history, but be a part of it too. But then, everyone thinks that when they're freshly twenty.

In retrospect, it was all somewhat of an illusion and we weren't actually standing on the cusp of anything unique or grand. We were college kids with smooth hands. We were horny for revolution just like every class before us, and like our predecessors, some of us graduated and went on to become lawyers while others became labor organizers. The important fact in all of this is that regardless of what happened afterward: the experience of shouting slogans, marching, and arguing with passers-by taught us something about ourselves, about the traditions of progressive struggle, and about the importance of maintaining faith in an unbelieving culture. We were too young to be cynical, too idealistic to feel old. It was *perfect*, and at the same time, so was *Mos Def & Talib Kweli Are Black Star*.

This wasn't protest music; these were songs of love and devotion for a generation that had lost its way and caught on with the wrong swagger. At the time—and trust me, it does seem like it was many hip-hop lifetimes ago—Black Star was like the Harlem Renaissance, the Black Panthers, and the Native Tongues rolled into one; it was the hopes and contradictions of twentieth-century life angled into multipurpose verse. Kweli was blessed with a subtlety of approach and punchy, breathy anxiety while Mos's childishly smooth voice and man-sized vision boomed with a weathered au-thority that betrayed his age. Their appearances on various Rawkus

12-inches positioned them at the vanguard, and their debut was supposed to be the poem, manifesto, slogan, anthem—*the everything*—of a generation.

The thing is, *Mos Def & Talib Kweli Are Black Star* really isn't a phenomenal album. For all its wonder and imagery—and you didn't have to be a dumb college kid to get this; it just seemed *special* at the time—the album is inconsistent and a little half-assed, never really finding the strut you expect. But it was filled with promise and it inspired belief, if not hope. Every generation gets that swell at some point—the need to *represent* and do good —but not every generation has a Mos Def and Talib Kweli.

Black Star was an ambitious album that arrived in the midst of hip-hop's late-1990s restructuring. The independent revolution proved unsuccessful as class, race, economy, and ambition fractured The Underground into a philosophy built on rejection and reaction. Aboveground producers like Mannie Fresh, Timbaland, and the Neptunes (as well as Dr. Dre and Eminem) started bringing interesting sounds to the radio, but progress—moral, not just material—seemed irrelevant. Through all of this, Mos Def and Kweli didn't shy away from the grand, great questions: What *is* hip-hop? and What *should* it be? It was love, theft, an old copy of *The Bluest Eye*, and a hand-me-down understanding of

Marcus Garvey's grand design for repa- triation to Africa in the early 1920s. Like Garvey, the man who christened his fleet the Black Star Liners, the ambition alone of Mos and Kweli's project counts for something. The album suggested deliverance and salvation not just for black folk, but for city dwellers, art cats, passionate souls, and human beings everywhere. As hip-hop was getting more and more micro, here came Mos Def and Talib Kweli with the universalism of love and experience.

The thrust of *Black Star* is summarized by Kweli on "K.O.S. (Determination)": "The most important time in history is NOW." It's a directive. It's an order to go out into the world and make better, to scribble down exactly who we be at this precise moment. The idealistic "Definition" and "RE:DEFinition" converged hip-hop's past—Boogie Down Productions' "P is Free" beat, the twin legacies of the late 2Pac and Biggie—into the vast, open space of the present—our present. "Brown Skin Lady" was a love song to the ideal of love, a rare beauty of a song about the innocence, bliss, and hokeyness of first flames and stardust. "Respiration" sat you down right next to Mos, Kweli, and guest Common on trains and stoops, taking in the jerky skylines anew with young, wide eyes. The album's poetic masterpiece was the stunning "Thieves in the Night," with lyrics about the narrow gaze of youth and the hard knocks of coming-of-age that were cribbed straight from Toni Morrison's *The Bluest Eye*. Despite several gaffes—most notably their choice to end the album with the punchless "Twice Inna Lifetime"— *Black Star* was still a great record with moments of pure, untouched idealism and, importantly, a want of vision.

Change would come and though it was natural, it wasn't what you would have expected (or hoped for) at the time. By the time they went on to do solo work in the following years, Mos and Kweli seemed a little jaded and weary of their overtly conscious stances. Though they would each release solo albums—Mos's *Black on Both Sides* and Kweli and producer Hi-Tek's collaborative *Reflection Eternal*—that were actually better than *Black Star*, they would never recapture the naïvely free vastness—the moment—of that first record. It was probably for the better. As hip-hop's turf wars and success confused even its staunchest disciples, Mos used his solo debut to warn that hip-hop, whatever it may be, will never save you. But, after youthful idealism surrendered to the control and pressures of maturity, was hip-hop itself still worth saving for them, for these self-christened "universal magnetic B-Boys"? Even once the *big* questions were tabled for us kids and the exuberance lost, the *idea* of those anxious, angsty fights still gives strength. In practice we fell short, just as *Black Star* does, but we learned the most important lesson of them all: Greatness is a means, not an end, and sometimes it pays to simply have the guts to think big. We'll get there eventually.

by Hua Hsu

Nas: Illmatic (Columbia, 1994)

Nas:
Illmatic

Hip-hop is a culture obsessed with heroes, and whether they're the result of manufacturing or earnest hard work, they're rarely as immovable as they think. A culture whose music and approach assume a short attention span necessarily treats its stars similarly, and the debate about hip-hop's truly untouchable names would be relatively short. The days of Nas's undisputed spot atop the dawg pile may be long gone, but he will always have his place in the discussion, not simply as a gifted lyricist, but as a prodigy.

Nas came into our world fully formed as a snot-nosed upstart, nonchalantly bragging that he "went to hell for snuffing Jesus" at age twelve. At the time he was a twenty-year-old counting stacks with partner AZ on "The Genesis," the weightily named introduction to his debut, *Illmatic*. The album has no moments of vulnerability, no rags to put the riches of today into proper perspective. He arrives a man-child in a broken land: a man because there is no adolescent uncertainty in his pose, but a child because it is so obviously and precisely a pose. As with many who inherit a precocious brain but a plain heart, he relies more on instinct and response than emotional certainty, conviction, or stability. It's as though the questions one wrestles in youth (about idealism, materialism, morality, "the future") didn't matter, for Nas arrived immortal.

As such, *Illmatic* is fearless, shocking, and literally *unbelievable*. There's a brazenness to Nas's "understandable smooth," yeah-I-said-it delivery, a cool absence of thought or hope (maybe both), and whether he was indeed the journal or the journalist, there were few images as crisp or brags as cold as his: "I never sleep, 'cause sleep is the cousin of death"; "'Cause I'm as ill as a convict who kills for phone time / ... / I rap in front of more ni**az than on the slave ships." On "One Love," his description of an overanxious young thug from around the way—"Shorty's laugh was cold-blooded as he spoke so foul / Only twelve trying to tell me that he liked my style / Then I rose, wiping the blunt's ash from my clothes / Then froze, only to blow the herb smoke through my nose" — wasn't just a dope rap lyric; it was an amazing piece of writing, regardless of the creator's age.

Through it all, Nas himself seems to seek very little in the exchange. If he is to be believed, he is already rich, and though he would later try to refashion himself as a martyr-in-progress, on *Illmatic* he seems too young and jaded to care much about any end because in the end, nothing happens. Do you find redemption in ether? Do you pray for a merciful God? No. Life's a bitch and then you die, and the only thing Nas seems to believe in is the grace of falling. Religion clearly doesn't matter ("'Cause yeah, we were beginners in the hood as Five-Percenters / But somethin' must of got in us 'cause all of us turned to sinners," he says on "Life's a Bitch") and when Nas boasts that he "loves committin' sins" (on "Represent"), you *almost* believe him.

Almost because there's still something behind Nas's eternally negative, harum-scarum worldview —not fear, but a dim consciousness of his own immortal status. It is the belief that though *we* may not live to see tomorrow, *someone* will. And with history as our witness, we'd better seem pretty

fucking fly to them. On *Illmatic*, Nas cares less about his place in God's eyes than his place in history, and history alone provides young Nas with a sense of salvation—that the depravity surrounding him would one day be enshrined as the conditions for his genius. The album, like the man himself, excels because it is obsessed with the bright, fawning legacy that trails faithfully behind. He says as much on "Nas Is Like," a song he wrote during the *Illmatic* sessions: "But what's it all worth? Can't take it with you under this Earth / Rich men died and tried, but none of it worked / They just rob your grave, I'd rather be alive and paid / Before my number's called, history's made."

There's something alluring and inevitably unsatisfying about seeing someone so nihilistic go about life, especially at such a young age. You can say you want to (or will) die before you get old, but those words feel cheap and flat when you live *just* cautious enough to survive well into your late twenties and early thirties. When you grow up against the ideals and wishes you lay out in the dim idealism of youth, you go from old school to old fool, and somewhere along the way, old Nas realized that he wanted redemption. He thought he would find it by earning the plaques and sales that he rightfully deserved, refashioning himself as a pretty thug and then again as a champion for the masses, finding solidarity with lesser cliques (Bravehearts, Murder Inc.), and beefing with Jay-Z, the man who took the best parts of Nas's blueprint and gave it both corporate and heartfelt dimensions. But nothing worked, and these muted expressions of fear only served to make *Illmatic* seem that much more unbeliev-able. As a kid, Nas didn't fear God; he just thought he was better, and he wanted people to know that tomorrow. Unfortunately, that next day came, and the boy who was ahead of his time grew into a man forever captive to it.

Notorious B.I.G.:

Ready to Die (Bad Boy/Arista, 1994)

Life After Death (Bad Boy/Arista, 1997)

by Jon Caramanica

Notorious B.I.G.:
Ready to Die

Notorious B.I.G.:
Life After Death

It didn't take very long at all for Christopher Wallace—aka Notorious B.I.G., Biggie Smalls, Frank White, etc.—to become the best rapper in the game. Asked once what pulled him away from his life as a small-time drug hustler in Brooklyn's Bedford-Stuyvesant neighborhood, Biggie scoffed, "A record deal," as if it couldn't have been more plain that one hustle could only truly be eclipsed by another.

When Biggie recorded the songs that would become his debut, *Ready to Die*, he wasn't more than a year removed from his street corner shenanigans. Call the result, then, an epic of magical realism. Better yet, the testament of a man enacting his will to power. There was plenty of darkness on the album, as there had been much darkness in his life. But *Ready to Die* raises a glass and toasts the possible, a triumph of tenacity and desire so profound it has yet to be matched on any other mainstream hip-hop album.

Biggie's hopes wouldn't have been possible without the intervention of Bad Boy Records founder Sean "Puffy" Combs. A cocksure young hustler, Puffy was an emperor in the making, needing a public face for his developing machine. He found it in Biggie, a decidedly affable guy who counterbalanced his imposing 300-something-pound frame with a disarming smile and a plethora of good cheer. By all accounts, Biggie was the exact opposite of what he appeared, and he made his career out of exploiting that perception/reception split.

Many of the best songs on *Ready to Die* come with no wink whatsoever, and Biggie's capacities for capturing the varying moods of the criminal mind are considerable. On "Warning," Biggie plays out both sides of an early-morning phone conversation, sometimes interrupting himself mid-bar to pick up the other narrative stream: "Call the coroner/There's gonna be a lot of slow slingin' and flower bringin'/ if my burglar alarm starts ringin'." This moment, like so many others on *Ready to*

Die, finds comedy in the grimmest subjects. He rarely explicitly pokes fun; more often, he illuminates the absurd moment with a turn of phrase so vivid—"Gimme the baby rings and the #1 MOM pendant," he tells a robbery mark—it renders the rest of the song moot.

Easy Mo Bee produced most of these tracks in his career-making moment. Crisp snares, thunderous bass, savvy soul—Easy Mo Bee created backdrops as syrupy as the rapper himself. However, the Puffy-coproduced songs that gave Biggie a foothold in the pop landscape presented him in a far different light. Puffy understood that America could be spoon-fed the hard core, but only if it had a sugar-sweet coating; he aimed for a middle ground somewhere between N.W.A.'s nihilism and MC Hammer's pop certitude.

To wit, Puff played up Biggie's unlikely sex appeal. The masterstroke was "One More Chance," both in its album version (a peppy, up-tempo bravado-thick riff) and in the remix (not included on the album), the version that would catapult the producer and his muse to worldwide fame. A delicious El Debarge sample set the mood, and Biggie dug in to spit hi-test game: "She sick of that song, on how it's so long / Thought he worked his until I handled my biz."

Just as great as his craving of pleasure was Biggie's gift for pain. Any conviviality on *Ready to Die* comes crashing to a close with the last track,

"Suicidal Thoughts." Biggie dials a friend, mumbles into the phone: "When I die, fuck it, I wanna go to hell / 'Cause I'm a piece of shit, it ain't hard to fuckin' tell." After a minute-long screed, there's a gunshot. The phone drops. A throbbing heartbeat brakes to a halt. *Ready to Die* opens with a birth and closes with a death, an entire life cycle crammed into seventy minutes.

Psychologically, no follow-up record was needed. When the double album *Life After Death* arrived just weeks after Biggie's murder in the spring of 1997, it couldn't help but feel bloated and indulgent, despite uniformly spineless critical adulation. It had to be asked: Biggie died for this? Art can ring trivial in the face of tragedy.

But it can also prove poignant. Push aside the obvious parallels between the cruel events that had just transpired and the album's pseudogoth aesthetic, and *Life After Death* revealed itself as one of hip-hop's first polyglot works. Rather than replicating the elements behind his initial success, Biggie pushed himself in new directions. His flow on *Life After Death* is markedly more intricate. He adopts unconventional rhyme patterns and highly detailed narrative styles, all matched by an affable pop sheen—making him perhaps the first rapper to improve his skills while becoming more popular.

Better, with the East-West wars at their apex, Biggie reached out a meaty hand to fans in all regions. "Nasty Boy" had Southern strip club appeal.

Bay Area pimps could relate to "The World Is Filled …," a Too $hort guest turn. Best of all was "Notorious Thugs," a partnership with Cleveland rap crooners Bone Thugs-N-Harmony, on which Biggie proved he could master even the most esoteric style.

On the one hand, it was shrewd marketing. By importing and staking claim to a whole range of sounds, Biggie ensured himself a whole host of listeners beyond the parochial New York scene. But that analysis overlooks the real lesson of the endeavor: No rapper other than Biggie had the skill to pull it off. It wasn't audacity, just creative roaming.

Biggie's travels also took him to the pinnacle of storytelling in rhyme, with a troika of songs that displayed both gravity and levity. "Niggas Bleed" grimly gives a first-person play-by-play of a drug exchange slowly going haywire, opening with a morbid warning: "All they tote is stainless / You just remain as calm as possible / Make the deal go through / If not, here's twelve shots / We know how you do." Despite its uniformly chilly tone, "Niggas Bleed" ends with a dash of light humor, with the enemy's car getting towed for being double-parked.

On "I Got a Story to Tell," the jokes continue. Seduced by a woman who's dating a member of the Knicks, Biggie is once again to work his sexual mojo. However, just after the deal is done—"I'm in his ass while he play against the Utah Jazz"—he and his partner are interrupted by the sounds of the baller returning home, ready for a romp. Thinking quickly, Biggie turns from lothario to thug, whipping out a gun and stealing the only thing the unsuspecting cuckold has left—money—before zooming away and immediately telling his friends, as any good bard should.

Finally, "Sky's the Limit" takes a wistful look back at an upbringing that began innocently and turned progressively wilder. The song would also give birth to the most moving tribute to the rapper following his death with its Spike Jonze–directed video. Jonze, an iconoclast revered in the skate world and known for his unconventional and irreverent treatments of pop songs, cast a pair of young Big and Puff look-alikes in a fantasy world where kids lived out the lives of their elders, ensuring they'd remain forever young. And more importantly, never die.

by Allen Gordon

N.W.A.: Straight Outta Compton (Ruthless/Priority, 1988)

N.W.A.:
Straight Outta Compton

N.W.A. will forever be associated with the terms "genocide," "misogyny," "nihilism," and "pathology." Though the group would happily market those social ills after Ice Cube's departure in 1990, in 1988, not one member of N.W.A. could have defined their music for a reporter using such descriptions. Questioning N.W.A. about their frivolous celebration of controversial behavior would closely resemble the famous 1971 exchange between heavyweight boxing champion Muhammad Ali and television reporter Howard Cosell:

COSELL: "Muhammad, you're being quite truculent today."

ALI: "Truculent? I don't know what that means, but if it's good … I'm it!"

After all, N.W.A. stood for "Niggas with Attitude," not "Niggas with Education." Yet like Ali, N.W.A. were brilliant in their own way even if they weren't scholars. What Eazy-E, Ice Cube, MC Ren, Dr. Dre, and DJ Yella lacked in academics, they more than made up for in poetic pontification on *Straight Outta Compton*. "You are now about to witness the strength of street knowledge," announces Dr. Dre on the album's intro, launching a salvo that offers what the group sees as more grass roots than anything ever heard before on record. And it is.

At the heart of N.W.A.'s dynamism is the different perspective each member brings to the same subject. Ice Cube and MC Ren usually wrote about their respective knowledge of gang activity from different vantage points. Ice Cube's rhymes were always explanatory and detailed; he was Rod Serling, explaining the whats, hows, and whys of the LA street criminal. His humorous and morally tragic view of the people orbiting drug dealers on "Dopeman" is part hero worship and part scathing critique. His verses, though spoken with anger and "attitude," are more of a teenager's facetious indictment of what the Black community has become since the infiltration of crack cocaine corrupted his politics of friendship, dating, and other elements of everyday life. This combination of condescension and myth-making characterizes his view of fellow South Central LA gang members ("Gangsta,

Gangsta" and "Straight Outta Compton"), alcoholism ("8 Ball"), and female corruption ("I Ain't tha One"). Ice Cube's didactic perspective can be summed up in one lyric from "Gangsta Gangsta": "Do I look like a muthafuckin' role model? / To a young kid lookin' up to me / Life ain't nothing but bitches and money."

MC Ren, on the other hand, isn't quite as amusing. Whereas Cube's boisterousness is menacing, Ren's sociopathic cool when calmly relating how murder by numbers raises a gang member's status is frightening: "Straight outta Compton, another crazy-ass nigga / More punks I smoke, yo, my rep gets bigger." Ren shows his fascination with hip-hop fans and his desire to be an emcee on his solo songs with Dr. Dre, "If It Ain't Ruff" and "Compton's in the House."

With Ice Cube and MC Ren laying the roadwork, Eazy-E could effortlessly become a mascot for N.W.A.'s image of hard core. Everything that was right and wrong about *Straight Outta Compton* was what created Eazy-E's record character and his real life. Like Ali, he wrote none of the poetry he spouted, relying instead on aides-de-camp: Ice Cube, MC Ren, and DOC. But Eazy made their words his own with an unmatched delivery on songs like "8 Ball" and "Parental Discretion Iz Advised." "He came off the best because he wasn't really serious about it," says Alonzo Williams. "The whole rapping thing and gangsta image was like a joke to him. He had fun with it." No small feat of theatrics, that.

"Fuck tha Police" is undoubtedly the album's showstopper due to its bold and scathing indictment of law enforcement's treatment of young Black males. Highlighted by Dr. Dre's crafty mock courtroom skit, each member's verse is a testimony to police brutality: Ice Cube is the teenager with no gang affiliation; MC Ren is the rebellious gang member; and Eazy-E is the criminal mastermind who finances police corruption only to be still subjected to the harassment his payments are meant to fend off. Ironically, the four rapping members of N.W.A.—Eazy-E, Ice Cube, MC Ren, and Dr. Dre—would only appear together as a group on three songs: "Straight Outta Compton," "Parental Discretion Iz Advised," and "Fuck tha Police." The album is more of a showcase for the members' individual or tandem talents rather than a collective, which may have foreshadowed the group's breakup.

The music, while brilliantly produced, is overpowered by the vocal performances, profanity, and shocking subject matter. Aping the production techniques of Public Enemy's Bomb Squad, Dre and Yella raised the bar higher, adding studio musicians to interpolate guitar riffs or synthesizer sounds that didn't translate through samples alone. Where Ice Cube and Eazy-E would enunciate with

Cali accents and stretch syllables to make words rhyme, Dre would direct the players to follow with ad-libs on guitar so the song would always be on the same rhythm. They'd also add sound effects like gunshots, women screaming, police sirens, and the lot, giving the album a surreal feeling that transported the listener into the Compton of N.W.A.'s description.

The last song on the album, "Something 2 Dance 2," is a metaphoric and symbolic end to *Straight Outta Compton*. The electronic bass–laden song marks the end of the Los Angeles techno-hop era and ushers in the age of gangsta rap. More importantly, it is a party away from all the social ills that have been laid out on the previous ten songs. Neither threatening nor pathological, "Something 2 Dance 2" is partying away from the social disenfranchisement, violence, and racism that defines the world *Straight Outta Compton* represents. It's a traditional brief escape for American Black folk in a world that seems nigh inescapable.

Organized Konfusion:

S/T (Hollywood Basic, 1991)

by Joseph Patel

Stress: The Extinction Agenda (Hollywood Basic, 1994)

Organized Konfusion:
S/T

Organized Konfusion:
Stress: The Extinction
Agenda

Each of Organized Konfusion's three albums were cast in varying degrees of tragedy and each time, the Queens duo emerged with works of art that belied hip-hop's typical emotional metabolism. There is rarely revelation of resonant fate with rappers and their street tales, but Pharaohe Monch and Prince Poetry made the machinations of anxiety—through rhymes of spirituality, mortality, and fantasy—part of their identity. They embraced the ephemeral and made the tenebrous tangible and called it their style.

Wunderkind white-boy producer Paul C was dead by the time Organized Konfusion was signed, but not before he helped to mold their soft-clay talent and ideology with his callous, beat-chopping fingers. Paul C didn't make it to the '90s, but the '90s wouldn't have made it without Paul C, and whatever innate rapping abilities Monch and Po had as aspiring art-school illustrators, Paul C honed it with his lawless vision behind the boards, which was only starting to bloom when he was killed in 1989.

Organized Konfusion's self-titled debut flaunts what he first taught them on the demo tape he produced—that the space to create is infinite—and by then, they had filled out into visionary form. Monch and Po spit, sang, slugged, and stuttered, which gave their rhymes a musical quality to match their instinctive lyrical observations. Paralleling the robust, bluesy bounce of "Fudge Pudge," Po introduces the group's creative treatise by augmenting his normal rhyming cadence with a dazzling array of seamless tricks: singing old soul riffs, busting out sound effects, mimicking the outgoing message of an answering machine, and, incredibly, crumbling the lyric sheet of an unsatisfying stanza only to start anew with another. This was Organized's modus operandi: each line was its own instrument valve to be blown through and played intrinsically to—and not, as is so often the case, independently of—the music.

Listen past the old-school harmonizing and call-and-response of "Walk into the Sun," and you find Monch trying to reap the hopeful from the destitute, a spiritual motif that courses through many Organized tracks: "In this particular era of darkness / Bust a rhyme that might enlighten the mind and spark this trail / to follow the light that's guiding you from the evil / as you walk into the sun." In the novel that is Organized Konfusion's story, Monch's finding-the-light-in-the-dark optimism foreshadows the energy he would need to draw when recording their follow-up album.

Arguably, the group's magnum opus was "Releasing Hypnotical Gases," a blast of afro-futurist sci-fi with an apocalyptic tenor appropriate for post–Persian Gulf War times. Recalling the assiduous mind of a young Rakim, the duo's spitfire visualization of chemical warfare molded together the anxiety of tricknology paranoia, the frustrations of socioeconomic inequality, and the eagerness of cultural rebellion into a slaying fantasy propelled by an urgent, bubbling soul-sonic force.

Organized Konfusion produced the entire debut album themselves, eschewing the then current conventions of production for a broader, organic sound that includes soul samples, live musicians, and even a Baptist church choir (thank you, Paul

C). In its attempt to lay out the entirety of Monch and Po's emotional spectrum, the album lacks cohesiveness. But that flaw is eclipsed by the album's sheer originality, and to celebrate it is to celebrate the group itself.

Stress: The Extinction Agenda, on the other hand, is the conceptual work Organized Konfusion always had in them. They more carefully calibrated this cryptically titled sophomore effort: thirteen songs were tightly woven into a sometimes savage, sometimes reflective exhumation of anxiety, emotion, and consequence. Organized used metaphor and escapism as an exercise of self-deliberation on their debut, but on *Stress* those mechanicals are even more finely tuned, and the result is an album of darker emission.

The specter hanging over *Stress* is the death of Monch's father, and by all indications the parent-child relationship was an interminably close one. There is other disquietude surrounding the album too, like the death of their artistic confidant, Hollywood Basic maestro Dave "Funken" Klein, and perhaps the duo's own uncertainty about a rapidly changing climate in the music industry that was beginning to favor demonstrative one-dimensionality over introspective exorcism. When the ghostly voices of the album's nebulous intro give way to Monch voicing his frustrations, it's really the rapper trying to find his place, not only as a disaffected black man in an unjust society, but also as a creative force in an unwelcoming genre and a fatherless son in a strange new world. Taking these factors into consideration, the vexation inherent in *Stress* becomes that much more poignant.

The group's storytelling amazes on "Stray Bullet," a lyrical exploration of the senselessness of black-on-black crime from the viewpoint of the assaulting bullet. The spiritual questions posed on "Why" and the pulpit-pitching on "Black Sunday" reveal personal vulnerabilities, but the duo's steadfast faith is ultimately assured on the closer, "Maintain." Rallying for a sense of community, "Let's Organize" hints at optimism, while "Thirteen" takes a nostalgic look at the group's youthful foundations. A mind-bending, acrobatic verbal display on "Bring It On" is Monch's superhero-like performance in defiance of the asthma that is his MC's Achilles' heel and the coup de grâce to his stylistic emergence on the album. In all, *Stress* has tremendous depth and purpose—the things one wants great art to possess—and this time, appreciation of the album goes beyond embracing the group's youthful ingenuity to include respecting it as a wonderful, thoughtful work of art.

Except that such things usually fall on deaf ears.

While their minds were still fired up enough to deliver an even more attuned concept album with *Equinox* (1996), their hearts knew better. *Equinox*, disappointingly, lacks inspiration. Maybe they sensed the sunset of their union was near, which had less to do with their own belief in each other and more to do with gravitational forces around them. What they discovered after the lukewarm reception to such a personal effort as *Stress* (though it was a critical and cult favorite) was that they were—and had always been—perhaps too creative for their own good. And that is the tragedy that clouds their third and final album: the death of Organized Konfusion itself.

OutKast:
Southernplayalisticadillacmuzik (La Face, 1994)
ATLiens (La Face/Arista, 1996)
Aquemini (La Face/Arista, 1998)
Stankonia (La Face/Arista, 2000)

by Tony Green

OutKast:
Southernplayalisti-
cadillacmuzik

OutKast:
ATLiens

Someone once said that advertising power is a substitute for actually having it. Which means the instant somebody opens their mouth to signify about themselves, they display impotence, not importance. Think about that when observing the rap game. There are more than a few whose boasts are statements of fact. But real power, more often than not, moves in stealth and exerts unseen force, like magnetism or gravity.

In the world of popular culture, power means affecting the dialogue without making it obvious. It means coaxing wider discussion into certain avenues, and steering it away from or blockading it in others. By this definition, it's clear that OutKast is pretty much the most powerful hip-hop force around. Start with its stunning record—four classic or near classic albums straight out the box—and go from there. But OutKast's most significant contribution to postmillennial pop music is their ability to affect the way people talk about it. With belief following discussion and perception following belief—how many VH-1 viewers think that the first half-century of American music wasn't a warm-up for rock 'n roll?—the importance of altering dialogue can't be overstated.

As of early 2000, there were certain things that you just couldn't say about hip-hop and pop music without at least pausing to drop in a "with the exception of OutKast" disclaimer, suggesting the preemption of a lot of stupid-assed shit. Were it not for Andre 3000 and Big Boi's stunning, Grammy-winning *Stankonia*, for example, the critical Stanley Crouches–in–training whining about the Britney-ization of pop music might have a point. So would all those mid-thirtyish alterna-dweebs who tossed all hip-hop on the "bling bling" junk pile while stumping for

Radiohead as the official repository of pop music intelligence. Not to mention the junior Bobo culture-site hacks who ground out master's theses on the earthshaking importance of two-step (insert here, in order, "intelligent drum 'n bass," "swing," and "acid jazz" and you've covered ten years of essaying on the cultural importance of white upper-middle-class club rats). Or to all those media and advertising types who regard said master's theses as the deciding factor in favor of a magazine-type "trend" story or the basis for an ad campaign. True, we're at an all-time low for mainstream cultural thinking, but imagine where the dialogue would be right now if some of these lines of reasoning hadn't been nipped in the bud. Fuckin' scary, huh?

Then there's the whole Southern hip-hop thing. Nearly fifteen years past the Geto Boys breakthrough and nearly seven into the post–Master P deluge, getting fans to acknowledge that Timbaland and the Neptunes prove that there are "some" good Southern rappers and producers is like pulling teeth. A conversation about the South will more likely spawn tired regional posturing, like blaming the Northern rappers' strip club aesthetic on a desire to please knuckle-dragging Southern buyers stupid enough to prefer Ludacris and Trick Daddy to N.O.R.E. That OutKast didn't completely redirect that dialogue says more about the dialogists than anything else. Applied to tunes like *Stankonia*'s "Ms. Jackson" and "B.O.B. (Bombs over Baghdad)"

or *Aquemini*'s "Rosa Parks" and "SpottieOttie-Dopaliscious," Northern hip-hop snobbery sounds less like aesthetic beef than desperate cries for Xanax.

Power. The same kind of power OutKast's spiritual forefathers (Parliament-Funkadelic) had, and continue to have. Both are the exception that proves the rule. P-Funk (and others like Earth, Wind & Fire) helped turn mainstream critical opinion on '70s black pop from dismissal—J. D. Considine once talked about how critics used to label the Isleys and Harold Melvin and the Blue Notes as "disco"—to overwhelming acceptance. Long after future retro-culture observers turn Mr. Cheeks and Nelly into poster children for a "shallowness of hip-hop" argument, OutKast will still be there to bitch slap them in the mouth.

Dre and Boi dropped *Southernplayalistica-dillacmuzik* at the tail end of a second hip-hop "golden age," a two-year period (1993–94) that spawned Wu-Tang's *Enter the Wu-Tang (36 Chambers)*, Snoop Dogg's *Doggystyle*, De La Soul's *Buhloone Mindstate*, Nas's *Illmatic*, and A Tribe Called Quest's *Midnight Marauders*. Like many albums released during that period, *Southernplayalistic* alluded to its roots (1200-sounding drums, turntable scratches, old-school hits, and tongue-twisting triplet verbalisms) while clearing the way for a new direction that used the peach cobbler soul funk of the Organized Noize production crew as a starting point. A year away from hitting mega-gold with TLC's "Waterfalls," Organized Noize presaged their future triumphs with tunes like the Bootsy-ish "Funky Ride." Dre and Boi's vision of Atlanta rang truer than the Afro-utopia of fellow Atlantans Arrested Development, or of jiggified popster Jermaine Dupri. Referencing both the black church and the Magic City and aided by members of Goodie Mob, Dre and Boi dropped "Dirty South" reality before the concept had even fully germinated in the mainstream hip-hop consciousness.

Sonically, they changed course on their next effort, 1996's *ATLiens*; the pair maintained the same perspectives as on their debut. This time out, they took a food share of production credit on "Jazzy Belle" and the signature "Elevators" ("Me and you, yo' mama and yo' cousin too"). The direction was presaged by the spooky "Ain't No Thang" off of *Southernplayalistic*. *ATLiens* followed that tune's textural implications down all kinds of dark, dub-influenced alleyways. Where *Southernplayalistic* was funky and hard-edged, *ATLiens* was dark, spacious, and narcotic ("Two Dope Boyz in a Cadillac") — syrup-sipping music before anyone outside of Houston had heard of DJ Screw.

Aquemini, the first album completely produced by OutKast, can be summed up by a line from "Liberation": "Can't worry about what another nigga think / Now see, that's liberation and baby I wants it." Not that they were worried—*Aquemini* was the album that almost nobody saw coming. *The Miseducation of Lauryn Hill* held it down for mainstream fans on the positivity tip, yo. Gang Starr endeared itself to heads longing for a sonic champion that returned to the days of the old boom-bap. And No Limit ruled everything below the Mason-Dixon. In this midst, Boi and Dre opened their third album with a vocals- and kalimba-spiced intro, went straight into a scorching broadside against anybody they could lay their hands on (from absentee fathers to crab-ass Southern Negroes), and then into a track dedicated to a Civil Rights–era icon ("Rosa Parks") spun around an acoustic guitar and blues harmonica.

Aquemini extended on many of the features of *ATLiens*. The Prince-ish piano of "13th Floor/ Growing Old" ran all through the wistful "Liberation." But here was an album that was more tuneful than the others, laced with patches of liquid guitar chording, eerie organ, and mournfully melodic basslines. Even more significantly, the crew—following the lead of compatriots Goodie Mob—continued to develop their shade tree philosophizing. "SpottieOttieDopaliscious" not only took the crew's dub jones to its logical conclusion, it featured what is arguably the duo's most pithy storytelling episode. Dre rhapsodizes over an episode of nightclub-spawned infatuation, while Big Boi finishes things up with a sobering exposition on life after the heat has gone: "Can't gamble feeding baby on that dope money / Might not always be sufficient / But the United Parcel Service… didn't call you back because you had cloudy piss / So now you back in a trap… / Go on and marinate on that…"

The near universal acclaim accompanying *Aquemini* (a five mic rating by *The Source*, a nine out of ten in *Spin*) was tough to follow, making the triumphant *Stankonia* even more impressive as it lorded over even *Aquemini* and *ATLiens*. The first single alone, "B.O.B. (Bombs over Baghdad)," was a stylistic tour de force, including crushing 808 bass frosted with Hendrixian guitars, organ, and gospel vocals—elements usually stretched out over the course of an album. Add some Westbound- era Funkadelic ("Stankonia [Stanklove]," "Slum Beautiful"), electro-Brazilia ("Humble Mumble"), pimp-preening funk ("So Fresh, So Clean," "We Luv Deez Hoez"), and molten funk-rock ("Gasoline Dreams"), and *Stankonia* becomes an album that could trump most full-lengths on its instrumentals alone. Here, though, Dre (now known as Andre 3000) and Big Boi delve even deeper into the details of life in the SWATS. "Ms. Jackson" is probably the most sensitive—and realistic—take on relationships to come out of hip-hop, while "Red Velvet" cautions would-be playas against pushing the floss envelope around "dirty boys" just waiting for a chance to add some gray flecks to that fur. And tunes like "Toilet Tisha" and "Slum Beautiful" reimagine 'round the way girls, not only as just more than one-dimensional accessories, but as objects of affection with lives and concerns that are worth exploring.

As this is being written, the duo is prepping a much-ballyhooed double album, something that is either a sign of overweening senses of importance (see The Smashing Pumpkins' *Mellon Collie and the Infinite Sadness*) or a genuine surfeit of dope shit. After hearing some of the stuff these fellas have in the can (and their coy hinting about the stuff that didn't make it onto *Stankonia* or former Dre paramour Erykah Badu's *Mama's Gun*), the latter option seems a safe bet. Bet you it pays off at 20-1, too.

OutKast:
Aquemini

OutKast:
Stankonia

by Ernest Hardy

Pharcyde: Bizarre Ride II the Pharcyde (Delicious Vinyl, 1992)

Pharcyde:
Bizarre Ride II
the Pharcyde

The Pharcyde's debut album, 1992's *Bizarre Ride*, is one of the most joyously heart-breaking records ever. Much of the sadness is contained within the music, where the complex issues of racial, artistic, and masculine identities (and authenticities) are couched in weed-drenched caps and wicked one-liners, and where razor-sharp observations are tucked into party anthems that—on the surface—ask nothing of you other than that you shake ya ass and nod ya head. But a lot of its sadness hovers on the periphery, in the heavy cultural baggage that has accumulated around being black, male, and a left-of-center artist in America. A lot of that central/peripheral blueness rests in the fact that with *Bizarre*, this LA-based outfit sprang fully formed into the world, but due to a combination of factors (stresses within the group, a music industry that didn't know what to do with them, how those two items fed one another), Pharcyde could not live up to the dazzling promise of their debut and eventually fizzled out.

This is an album that should have been a huge commercial success instead of the cult item that it became, but it was too effortlessly an affront to too much "conventional wisdom" for that to happen. At the time it was released, it deftly exploded many of the clichés and stereotypes that were (and still are) being uncritically embraced, celebrated, and bought elsewhere in hip-hop. And that, in part, is what doomed *Bizarre Ride*.

Bizarre is a West Coast album that isn't about gangs or overly familiar blood-and-violence-soaked hood narratives; it's an Afro-Bohemian album with pointed racial consciousness. But it's also self-deprecating about that consciousness, honest about the pain and anxiety that such awareness can bring. It pulls lacerating humor out of the stuff of despair and then floats on a cloud of black-boy giddiness, where Negroes can trip on their own cleverness and wit. And though the album is thickly laced with samples, it doesn't pander, doesn't use overly familiar, nostalgic sound cues as a crutch to mask a lack of vision or artistry.

The sly wit and devastating insight of their lyrics are summed up perfectly on the musical skit "Jigaboo Time." The body of the song is a recitation of all the ways in which black folk shuck and jive, play themselves in order to get some play and get paid, and it's a clear indictment of the practice: "Yo, when you rappin' for the money, it's jigaboo time (what?) / It's jigaboo time (what?), it's jigaboo time / ... / When you don't have soul, it's jigaboo time / It's jigaboo time, it's jigaboo time." But the punch to the gut comes with the two lines that bookend the piece, the opener ("When you sign across the line, it's jigaboo time / It's jigaboo time (yo what?), it's jigaboo time") and the devastating closer ("But we're all jigaboos — in our owwwwwwn wayyyyyy / So, might as well just get paid and say, fuck it, y'know"). The opening line is acknowledgment of the fact that black folk are expected to "perform" from the door, like it or not, and that's a fact that has to be negotiated daily. The closing line owns up to the ways in which we actually conform to that expectation, consciously or not, with the final phrase summing up the resignation that passes for enlightenment and twenty-first-century Negro pragmatism, as embodied by the bottomless materialism that has taken hold of rap music.

That's not to say that there aren't moments where humor ain't nothing but humor ("Ya Mama," the hilarious ode to the dozens) or where the party ain't nothing but a party ("Soul Flower," which reworks James Brown's "Soul Power" into an impossibly infectious, funky Afro-Boho anthem). But what makes the album resonate after all these years is the multihued quilt of emotions and politics, escapist thrust and inescapable reality. It's just real.

Public Enemy:
It Takes a Nation of Millions to Hold Us Back (Def Jam, 1988)
Fear of a Black Planet (Def Jam, 1989)

by Peter Shapiro

Public Enemy:
It Takes a Nation of
Millions to Hold Us Back

Public Enemy:
Fear of a Black Planet

Hip-hop purists will tell you it was Run-D.M.C., historians will tell you it was the Cold Crush Brothers, crate diggers will you it was A Tribe Called Quest, nihilists will tell you it was N.W.A., alternative-culture hounds will tell you it was Ultramagnetic MCs, frat boys and the Anti-Defamation League will tell you it was the Beastie Boys, and crackers will tell you it was Insane Clown Posse, but identity politics and petty genre squabbles aside, there can be no doubt that the greatest hip-hop group ever was Public Enemy.

PE made hip-hop the most vital cultural form of the last twenty-five years and made everybody from college professors to lunkhead guitarists come to terms with the genre. They may have attracted the most controversy for their embrace of the Nation of Islam's teachings and some poorly considered words from Professor Griff, but with rapper Chuck D's fervid, forceful, stentorian boom and the Bomb Squad's radical sonics, they would have attracted notoriety even if they had been supporters of Billy Graham.

Public Enemy came together in the early '80s around Bill Stephney's radio show on WBAU. Stephney was soon joined by Hank and Keith Boxley (later Shocklee) and graphic design student Carlton Ridenhour (aka Chuck D). With DJ Terminator X, Minister of Information Professor Griff, and hype man Flavor Flav in tow, Public Enemy caught the ears of Def Jam's Rick Rubin and signed to the label in 1987. Produced by the Bomb Squad (the Shocklees and Eric Sadler), their first album, *Yo! Bum Rush the Show* (1987), was the sound of a group just finding its feet. Nonetheless, it hinted at a group with prodigious talent.

Nineteen ninety-eight's *It Takes a Nation of Millions to Hold Us Back* is hip-hop's greatest album and one of popular music's true masterpieces. No punk or speed metal album has harnessed the power of chaos and rage as effectively; no "folk" album has been as articulate in its anger; no reggae or gospel album has been as righteous; no avant-garde album has been as experimental *and* as coherent. Only James Brown has made a record as electric as "Bring the Noise" or "Night of the Living Baseheads," and no one has managed the trick of making a record that is as simultaneously tense and rousing as "Black Steel in the Hour of Chaos." Even as the album's wild samplescapes and radical black nationalism have become old hat over the ensuing years, *It Takes a Nation of Millions to Hold Us Back* remains as exciting, visceral, and galvanizing as it was when it first came out.

Chuck D embraces Farrakhan, criticizes urban radio for backing away from the group's pro-black politics, slams drug dealers, declares that he's "an un-Tom," breaks out of prison, gives the finger to the National Association of Recording Arts and Sciences, and sprays militant graffiti over the FBI building. On "Bring the Noise," he neatly summarizes hip-hop's aesthetic and why it's so radical in a few words: "Whatcha gonna do? Rap is not afraid of you / Beat is for Sonny Bono, beat is for Yoko Ono / ... / Wax is for Anthrax, still it can rock bells."

Of course, protest music is only ever as effective as the music itself, and only a handful of artists —Sly Stone, James Brown, Parliament, the Velvet Underground—have so perfectly matched music and words. Swarming with feedback drones, James Brown horn riffs turned into air-raid sirens, shards of thrash metal guitar, white noise, disembodied chants, motive scratching, crowd noise from a concert in London, plastic bass bombs, and breakbeats turned into war drums, *It Takes a Nation of Millions to Hold Us Back* is the riot in Cellblock #9 committed to wax. But for all the agitprop, it was still as funky as hell: even though the samples (from the JBs, The Lafayette Afro-Rock Band, Isaac Hayes, etc.) were stripped of their context and had acid poured all over them, the grooves remained. "Louder Than a Bomb" sampled and borrowed the dynamics of Kool & The Gang's "Who's Gonna Take the Weight," and Flav threw around surrealist asides like Richard Pryor in a Dali landscape.

The homophobic and anti-Semitic bullshit of Professor Griff got the group in trouble with the media, and the spotlight only intensified with the release of the incredible, Elvis-dissing "Fight the Power" (1989), which many commentators read as an incitement to violence. Riding a bouncing but menacing JB bassline, "Fight the Power" was indeed PE at their most rousing, and may be the best articulation of their equation of raw funk and militancy. The group's response to the controversy surrounding the single was the absolutely stunning "Welcome to the Terrordome." Perhaps the most radical, uncompromising single ever to achieve significant sales, "Welcome to the Terrordome" was the Bomb Squad at their most amelodic, intense and seething. Like many of hip-hop's biggest celebrities, PE were wracked by paranoia, but instead of wallowing in it like Biggie or Tupac, they projected it outward on this savage, vicious, caustic, and breathtaking jeremiad.

Both songs were included on 1990's *Fear of a Black Planet*, which was just as incendiary, and in its own way just as awesome as *It Takes a Nation*, even if it lacked the previous album's head-spinning sonic invention. Inevitably, though, there was nothing else on the album that was as jaw-dropping or invigorating as "Fight the Power" or "Terrordome." *Fear* was a darker, less immediate album than *It Takes a Nation*: the title track was a disjointed, almost dubby song in favor of miscegenation that lurched across four or five different tempos; "Anti-Nigger Machine" was submerged in a queasy bassline; "Reggie Jax" was another deracinated, deconstructed reggae track that just barely crawled along; and Chuck D rapped "Pollywana-craka" in a deathbed style, parodying "Quiet Storm" DJs. Cloaked in resignation and frustration and bitterness and moving at a brutal, bruising pace that just ground on and on, *Fear* was almost hip-hop's version of Sly Stone's *There's a Riot Goin' On*, Funkadelic's *Maggot Brain*, or the Rolling Stones' *Exile on Main Street*.

When it did decide to become engaged, though, *Fear* was galvanic. "911 Is a Joke" was Flavor Flav's star turn—the court jester becomes politically savvy. "B Side Wins Again" managed to stir the troops despite the murky production. "Who Stole the Soul" was another street riot in the style of "Terrordome." Then there was the fiery "Burn Hollywood Burn," which featured three of hip-hop's most powerful voices —Chuck D, Ice Cube, and Big Daddy Kane—bringing the noise on celluloid racism.

Fear, however, was effectively the end for PE. The result of antisampling litigation, group turmoil, and coming too close to the brink one too many times, the group's fourth album, *Apocalypse 91… The Enemy Strikes Black*, was a definite retreat, even if it was better than 99 percent of everything else that was around at the time. A series of very average recordings followed, and since hip-hop is so ruthless—if you miss a step and fail to keep up for even a second, it swallows you whole—the music's standard-bearers fell victim to the very thing that made their genre so vital.

by Lefty Banks

V/A: Return of the DJ (Bomb Hip-Hop, 1996)

V/A:
Return of the DJ

By the early 1990s, the DAT all but made the DJ DOA. The previous generation had a much different relationship with DJs given equal—if not top—billing with MCs (e.g., Jazzy Jeff and the Fresh Prince, Eric B & Rakim, et al.). Moreover, rap albums regularly included at least one or two DJ tracks, be it Eric B's "Chinese Arithmetic" on *Paid in Full* or "Mister Cee's Master Plan" on Big Daddy Kane's *Long Live the Kane*. This trend radically changed with the coming popularity and affordability of Digital Audio Tapes. The DAT eliminated the cost and hassle of bringing DJs on tour, and let rappers bask solo in the glow of the marquee. And the death of the disc jockey wasn't limited to the music industry. The world Disco Mix Competition (DMC), a yearly contest to determine the world's best DJs, had largely become a showcase for gimmicky body tricks rather than artistic or technical brilliance. On several fronts, the once-grand adventures on the wheels of steel were steadily grinding to an ignominious halt.

But DJing hadn't disappeared; it had simply retreated back underground, and while the rest of the hip-hop nation indulged its mic fetishes, DJs across the country continued to innovate and waited for the opportunity to return full force. Led by wax wizards like San Francisco's Invisibl Skratch Piklz, LA's Beat Junkies, and New York's X-Ecutioners (then called the X-Men), DJs reinvented their role. No longer just the sideshow attraction, they now flexed enough artistic muscle to be the main attraction.

Assembled by Bomb Hip-Hop Records' founder Dave Paul, the *Return of the DJ* didn't discover a scene so much as it made it visible to the larger world. For example, by the time of the album's release in 1996, the Invisibl Skratch Piklz, long considered the world's most talented DJ team, had already retired from active competition. But for many who didn't religiously watch DMC battle tapes, *Return* was the first time they ever heard one of those routines committed to a recording. In that respect, *Return* helped scratch DJing move beyond being mere auditory accessory (i.e., a ziggy-zig hook on a chorus) into the realm of budding artistry (i.e., a DJ-composed routine that doubled as a full-length song).

On the surface, the new scratch DJing—dubbed "turntablism" by the Beat Junkies' DJ Babu—paid homage to the pioneering work that preceded it, cuts like Gang Starr's "DJ Premier Is in Deep Concentration," Jazzy Jeff's "A Touch of Jazz," or the aforementioned progenitor of it all: Grandmaster Flash's seminal "Adventures on the Wheels of Steel." But with scratch patterns as intricate as a Charlie Parker horn line or a Roy Haynes breakbeat, the album's participants raised the bar for DJ virtuosity. At one end were songs like DJ Ghetto's "Ghetto on the Cut" or Kool DJ E.Q.'s "Death of Hip-Hop"—mostly a pastiche of different scratches laid over a single, self-produced beat. At the other end was the Piklz' "Invasion of the Octopus People," which had DJs Q-Bert, Shortkut, and Disk channeling the group synergy of a jazz trio, with each member playing percussion, bassline, or melody—literally constructing an entire song from scratching alone.

Other precedents: the X-Men's Rob Swift recording one of his popular juggling routines for "Rob Gets Busy," resplicing everything from the JBs' "Blow Your Head" to Biz Markie's "Nobody Beats the Biz"; Jurassic 5's Cut Chemist offering his follow-up on Double Dee and Steinski's groundbreaking cut 'n paste series, "Lessons 1–3," with "Lesson 4," an ode to hip-hop radio; and Peanut Butter Wolf paying tribute to over fifteen years of hip-hop history with the incredible "The Chronicles (I Will Always Love Her)," a montage of musical snippets beautifully stitched together. Read the rest of the roster and *Return* looks like a prescient DJ all-star lineup: Mixmaster Mike, Z-Trip, and Babu submit solo cuts, plus there's a provocative collaboration between Japan's Yukata and Honda with pioneering LA DJ legend Aladdin.

The most telling aspect of the album's impact is in how much turntablism has changed in the scant years that followed *Return*'s 1996 release. Even by the series' third volume in 1999, much of the scratching on the first volume feels almost anachronistic, especially compared to the hyper-complex styles that most DJs now boast. This evolution takes away nothing from the singular achievement of *Return of the DJ*, which was as complete a snapshot as one could take of the turntablism scene right at its breakout moment.

by Chris Ryan

The Roots: Things Fall Apart (MCA, 1999)

The Roots:
Things Fall Apart

In a time when Pen and Pixel was the dominant motif for album covers, they had a black-and-white photo of a burned out church. In a time when Swizz Beats' honking drum machine reigned supreme, they had a real kit tuned to mimic Marley Marl's snare cracks. In a time when most rap shows were little more then glorified advertisements for product, they were the best live band in hip-hop, a democratic group in a genre where the star was king. And in a time when most of their peers concentrated on making a few singles with lavish videos and then padded discs with filler, they made an album with one cohesive statement. In 1999, The Roots went back to the future.

Things Fall Apart shot down all the misconceptions anyone had about a bunch of guys from Philly, most of them graduates from a performing arts high school who had a live-rap band. It broke The Roots out of all the pigeonholes anyone could put them into. The album is funny, raging, aggressive, melodic, experimental, and pop. It wasn't jazz-rap or alternative hip-hop. It wasn't for the streets or the college dorms. It was too precise, too unique for any of that.

Before this particular album's release, the group had never quite captured the sound or feeling of their explosive live show on tape; the anything-can-happen-ness was missing. Previous long-players like *Organix, Do You Want More?,* and *Illadelph Halflife* were all solid affairs that showed off the respective and bountiful skills of the group's players. But the recordings were somewhat muted by the band's inexperience with recording. With *Things Fall Apart,* The Roots found a secret weapon, a tool to flesh out their ideas and represent the visceral nature of the band: they learned how to use the studio.

Things Fall Apart marked the emergence of The Roots, their point of musical maturity. It showcased drummer Ahmir "?uestlove" Thompson as a musical mind and Black Thought and Malik B as lyricists, not to mention the band's ability to navigate tradition (old-school hip-hop, classic soul flourishes) with the here and now (drum 'n bass, sound collages, unconventional song structures). Most rap records in 1999 started with plodding intro tracks on which the artist would announce his arrival, warn his haters, and shout out his fam. *Things* starts with a sound clip from Spike Lee's *Mo' Better Blues*, a scene where two jazz musicians played by Denzel Washington and Wesley Snipes argue, basically about selling out and keeping it real. Hearing these first thirty seconds, you had to know something was up.

"Table of Contents (Parts 1 & 2)" is the album's jumping-off point. Immediately it's ?uestlove's drums—distorted, fading in and out. It brings on a memory flash: it's 1989 and you're up way past your bedtime trying to get a late-night rap radio show from God knows where on your crappy bedside radio, and somewhere on the airwaves a man is dropping science on a funky drummer. Black Thought has that beat in his stomach: "The mic chord is an extension of my intestine."

"The Next Movement" has a backsliding snare and the elegant accompanying coos of the Jazzyfatnastees as the spoonful of sugar. Black Thought has the medicine: "Yo, the whole state of things in the world 'bout to change / Black rain fallin' from the sky look strange / The ghetto is red-hot, we stepping on flames." On "Step into the Realm,"

?uestlove's drums are mixed to imitate the fading breaks of a pause-play loop from his youth. I'm probably as old as ?uestlove, and the bass rumble and mic mathematics never sounded anything like this in *my* youth.

As forward-thinking off the record as they are on it, The Roots took advantage of their (till that point) mild success to introduce many people to the extended musical family they had fostered. Detroit production guru Jay Dee mapped out the soulful atmosphere of "Dynamite." D'Angelo added keys to the jazzy "The Spark." The songwriting, production, and keyboards of Philly homeboys Scott Stortch and James Poyser are present throughout the album, while Philly homegirls Jill Scott and Eve (then known as Eve of Destruction in her short-lived Dr. Dre apprenticeship) added their distinctive voices on the certified hit "You Got Me." Along with other guests such as Common and Ursula Rucker, the band created a living, breathing community that is still producing stellar records to this day (check the okayplayer.com website). Aimed both at the state of the world and the state of the music they thought was deteriorating in front of their very eyes, The Roots, with a little help from their friends, a lot of courage, soul by the pound, and skill by the gallon, took a few steps towards putting things back together.

Run-D.M.C.:

S/T (Profile/Arista, 1984)
King of Rock (Profile/Arista, 1985)
by David Toop
Raising Hell (Profile/Arista, 1986)

Run-D.M.C.:
S/T

Run-D.M.C.:
King of Rock

Run-D.M.C.:
Raising Hell

By 1984, the year in which *Run-D.M.C.* was released on Profile, the Hollis, Queens, trio—rappers Joseph Simmons and Darryl McDaniels and DJ Jason "Jam Master Jay" Mizell—had already made their mark on the old school. Their first 12-inch tracks, "It's Like That/Sucker M.C.'s" and "Hard Times/Jam Master Jay," cut across the electro sound still dominating clubs like The Funhouse in 1983, slowing down the tempo, toughening up the beats, and bringing a more aggressive, grittier style to their rhymes and flow.

Run-D.M.C. could have followed the pattern of most rap albums up until that point: singles + filler. However, Run-D.M.C. and manager Russell Simmons were too conscious of the group's future potential to be complacent. From their dressed-down outfits of black leather, track suits, and trilbies to the sparse sound of their backing tracks, they made a clean break with the past. Produced by Orange Krush member Larry Smith and Russell Simmons (Joseph's older brother), the debut album opened with "Hard Times." Building on the success of protest raps like "The Message" by Grandmaster Flash & the Furious Five, "Hard Times" was part of this movement, yet the music sounded as uncompromising as the lyrics.

Larry Smith's approach to the music was to create simple beats—mostly kick drum, snare, and claps—using the fat sounds of an Oberheim DMX drum machine. A one-note bassline would be tied to the kick drum, with the only variation coming from minimal touches of percussion, sound effects, and Jam Master Jay's scratches. The exceptions to this rule appeared on "Rock Box" and "30 Days." Anticipating their 1986 collaboration with Aerosmith, "Rock Box" was smothered in Eddie Martinez's metal guitar hysteria, while keyboards and harmonizer effects gave extra spice to the witty lyrics of "30 Days."

Although Run-D.M.C. sounded hard for their time, their rhymes were full of humor and catch phrases ("It's like that and that's the way it is") that stuck in the memory. On "Sucker M.C.'s," Joe and Darryl took turns with lengthy raps, but also switched to their trademark style of alternating lines, parts of lines, and even single words between them. By the release of their second album, *King of Rock*, any trace of uncertainty had been whipped out of the mix. The bare drum machine and echo-delayed vocals of "Rock the House" led into the irresistible rock/rap fusion of the title track. Eddie Martinez played guitar again, but his sound had moved from AOR screaming to the raw brutality of AC/DC riffs. For better or worse, *King of Rock* was the template for Limp Bizkit's nu-metal.

The balance of songs was similar to the first album: Jam Master Jay catches praise on "Jam Master Jammin'"; "You Talk Too Much" is a moral sermon with keyboards added; "Can You Rock It Like This" reprises Martinez's guitar format; "Daryll and Joe" is straight-ahead freestyling over 808 drum blasts and Jay's scratching; "It's Not Funny" is full of quirky jokes about the cruelty of life; and "Roots, Rap, Reggae" is exactly what its title suggests. One of the most interesting tracks on the album is "You're Blind," a slow protest rap in the "Hard Times" mold. With Def Jam Records founder Rick Rubin playing one of the distorted guitars, the song has a feel heavy enough to recall Led Zeppelin's power.

Rubin's influence was growing fast and by 1986 he had taken over for Larry Smith as Run-D.M.C.'s coproducer, resulting in *Raising Hell*, which Russell Simmons called the first "b-boy album." Out went the keyboard decoration, vocal reverb, and any other pretense of commercialism. The vocals were more aggressive than ever, Jam Master Jay cut savage bursts of noise, and the subject matter of tracks like "Son of Byford" and "Born to be Black" showed Joe and Daryll aiming for a new level of seriousness.

Among its other innovations, *Raising Hell* was one of the first hip-hop records to prominently feature an old-school break, Bob James's "Mardi Gras" on "Peter Piper." It was also one of the first in a very long line to use the word "motherfucker." Rubin plays fuzz guitar for "Raising Hell," and "You Be Illin'" is comedy R&B in the style of The Coasters, a reminder that Russell Simmons was well aware that hip-hop's place was in the African-American musical tradition. The two most significant tracks on the album, however, are "My Adidas" and "Walk This Way."

Not just a song of praise to their sneakers, "My Adidas" protested against stereotyping somebody for the shoes they wear. Inevitably, as Run-D.M.C. became the most successful hip-hop act of their time, Adidas took on sponsorship of their stadium tours. For "Walk This Way," Rubin persuaded Steve Tyler and Joe Perry of Aerosmith to play on the reworked version of the song. The result was a breakthrough for hip-hop into the predominantly white MTV audience. It could be argued that this single track could take a large part of the credit for hip-hop's overwhelming commercial success in the late '90s.

Run-D.M.C. have never matched the innovation and energy of these first three albums, though they continue to record, tour, and earn respect as musical pioneers—a tradition brought to a tragic end with the fall 2002 murder of Jam Master Jay in Queens, NYC, the city of his birth, life, and, ultimately, death.

by Todd Inoue

Slick Rick:
The Great Adventures of Slick Rick (Def Jam, 1989)

Slick Rick:
The Great Adventures
of Slick Rick

Y'all tucked in? Heeere we gooo ...

Couture: Bally shoes, Kangol hat, Gucci underwear, fly green socks. Toiletries: Johnson's Baby Powder, Oil of Olay, Polo Cologne, fingernail file. Accessories: diamond-crusted eye patch, gold fronts, iced-out rings and knuckles, enough dooky ropes to choke a horse.

Slick Rick's obsession with flash and fashion may seem commonplace today, but when Adidas were the kicks of choice back in the '80s, Slick Rick generated an air of upper-crust sophistication by name-dropping labels. Like his distinct voice, which joined a British lilt and a Bronx accent, Slick Rick bridged hip-hop and the Hamptons with his narrative skills and rapier wit—the finest storytelling rhymer of all time.

Slick Rick (aka Ricky Walters, aka the Grand Wizard, aka MC Ricky D) arrived in the Bronx via Wimbledon, England, at age fourteen. He soon met up with Doug E. Fresh at a rap contest in 1984 and together, the duo would rock the parks and cut one of the most lethal double-sided blasts in hip-hop: "The Show/La Di Da Di." The latter, a humorous yarn ripped to Doug E. Fresh's tripled-up beat-box, gave a running commentary of Rick's day-in-the-life two decades before reality TV.

"La Di Da Di" set the tone for what would follow: Slick Rick's lasting monument to hip-hop, *The Great Adventures of Slick Rick*. Propelled by Slick Rick's own production work with partner Vance Wright and help from the Bomb Squad and Jam Master Jay, the album sealed Rick's reputation as a master of words and syntax. Many of the songs begin with a call to form a circle on the floor—à la kindergarten, not Rock Steady. "Gather 'round partygoers as if you're still livin'," he begins on "The Ruler's Back," "And get on down to the old Slick rhythm." Storytime was in full effect.

The songs on *Great Adventures* were sketches of street life that were either cautious warnings or glorified hedonism, depending on Rick's mood. "The Moment I Feared" puts listeners in Rick's Bally shoes as he is accosted for his jewels, engages in a ménage à trois and is caught by one of the lovers' boyfriend, and is finally sent to prison where he is gang raped. "Mona Lisa" is about a whirlwind flirtation and has an introduction worthy of a British monarch, complete with regal horn blasts. Rick introduces himself, his rapping partner (himself), and bows before himself to kiss his own ring. His dual personality continues on "Teacher, Teacher" and "Kit (What's the Scoop)," where he hits his own punch lines to excellent effect.

The album's high point, "A Children's Story," is a dark, surreal tale of repentance told through a bedtime story. Rick tucks his nephews into bed and freestyles his own version of *Goodnight Moon*. A seventeen-year-old robs the folks in the neighborhood, escapes from a cop, ducks into a crack house, holds a pregnant woman hostage, and is shot by police. "This ain't funny so don't you dare laugh / Just another case 'bout the wrong path / Straight 'n narrow or your soul gets cast / Goodnight!" The kids are left mumbling in disillusionment — "That Uncle Ricky, he sure is weird!"

As groundbreaking and amazing as that song is, *Great Adventures* isn't perfect. The lead cut, "Treat Her Like a Prostitute," is deemed an "oldie but goodie," but is positively Cenozoic in its view of women. " … all they do is hurt and trample," he grouses before warning, "Don't treat no girlie well until you're sure of the scoop." "Indian Girl—An Adult Story" is a freaky nursery school rhyme about Davy Crockett's encounter with Runny Rabbit and her talking box. He counters these X-rated moves with "Hey Young World," a "do as I say, not as I do" message song, and "Teenage Love," a slow jam that shows Rick closing with an interpolation of Diana Ross's "Do You Know Where You're Going To?"

The impact of Slick Rick and *Great Adventures* can be felt in the rhymes of Nas, Tupac, Biggie, Jay-Z, Foxy Brown, E-40, and Snoop Dogg (who covered "La Di Da Di") among others. Both Montell Jordan and Black Star used "A Children's Story" as a sample source for their own respective hits "This Is How We Do It" and "Children's Story." *Great Adventures* is still bumped, respected, and felt today as it was in 1988. Despite lukewarm response to follow-ups—as well as a ten-year stint in the pokey for attempted murder—Slick Rick will always be remembered for his *Great Adventures*, an essential b-boy document.

<u>by Mosi Reeves</u>

V/A: Solesides' Greatest Bumps (Quannum, 2000)
DJ Shadow: Endtroducing (Mo' Wax, 1996)

V/A:
Solesides'
Greatest Bumps

DJ Shadow:
Endtroducing

From 1993 to 1997, a small independent record company formed by several UC Davis college students—Josh "DJ Shadow" Davis, Xavier "Chief Xcel" Mosley and T. J. "Gift of Gab" Parker of Blackalicious, Lyrics Born, Lateef "the Truth Speaker" Daumont, and Jeff "DJ Zen" Chang—released one album, a CD of remixes, two EPs, and six 12-inch singles. The label never sold enough copies of their recordings to earn any gold or platinum plaques, and it exerted little to no influence on mainstream rap music and its now infamous "jiggy" era. But for five years, it established an alternate distribution system that upset the major labels' stronghold on record retailers by using independent distributors like Nu Gruv Alliance and TRC. Its business model has since been adopted by like-minded collectives such as Anticon, Rhymesayers, Def Jux, Galapagos 4, and dozens of other little-known upstarts.

But artistically, the Solesides discography is surprisingly inconsistent, considering its posthumous reputation as one of the most important labels of the '90s. One highlight was "Fully Charged on Planet X," a 12-inch single producer Chief Xcel recorded with Lateef and Gift of Gab that propels along the duo's quick-witted rhymes. Meanwhile, the brilliant "Latyrx" single paired Lateef with Lyrics Born over Shadow's sun-dazed dub, double-tracking the two MCs' voices at once into a dizzying sound clash. Other releases were less impressive. Lateef's "The Wreckoning" single droned on for two minutes as the Truth Speaker ladled out quips ("Those lyrics are so butt they must be synonymous with your behind") before climaxing with a horrific account of a dead MC's body deteriorating in its afterlife ("The flesh decomposes fast / Veins and skin turn purple, blue, green, and black").

Thankfully, the Solesides' *Greatest Bumps* compilation pulls out the label's diamonds in the rough (with Blackalicious' fiery freestyle marathon "Deep in the Jungle," a particular highlight), confirming the appeal of their freewheeling approach to conceptual hip-hop. Less didactic than Freestyle Fellowship yet not as accomplished as Organized Konfusion, the quintet produced brilliant rough drafts of songs that had charisma to spare but little polish. Many of Solesides' releases were, according to Chang's liner notes on the authoritative *Greatest Bumps* compilation, "the sum of its influences—Bounty Killer, Too $hort, Freestyle Fellowship, Art Farmer, Mickey and the Soul Generation, and hundreds of forgotten funk bands," distinguished by an enthusiasm and raw energy that eschewed artifice and condemned them to remain below the radar screen.

So when DJ Shadow boldly subtitled Solesides' debut single "Entropy (Part A—The Third Decade: Our Move," the group's "move" was mostly an invisible one, at least to the millions of heads who spent the mid-'90s watching the burgeoning rap industry nearly self-destruct from an overhyped East Coast/West Coast feud. Most of Shadow's work as a producer for Solesides consisted of minimalist beats for the MCs (Blackalicious' "Swan Lake," built around a cover version of the Stylistics' "People Make the World Go 'Round") and fun cut-and-paste adventures ("Hardcore [Instrumental] Hip-Hop") similar to the "DJ tools" tracks New York beatmakers like

Kenny "Dope" Gonzales were churning out at the time. Tacked on near the end of "Entropy," however, was "DJ Shadow's Theme," a disorienting, agonizingly slow waltz of drum loops and one ominous orchestral build-up. Obliquely minimalist, its then revolutionary approach sowed the seeds for Shadow's pioneering work in instrumental hip-hop (then called "trip-hop" by overzealous rock journalists).

Shadow continued to develop his ideas on two subsequent 12-inches for Mo' Wax—"Influx/Hindsight" and "What Does Your Soul Look Like?"—both of which found him ingeniously changing drum patterns on his tracks every eight bars and collating his rhythms with left-field samples that transformed his songs into soul-searching epics. By the time he released *Endtroducing* in late 1996, Shadow had evolved into a formidable sound artist, creating a veritable symphony out of long-forgotten breaks and fusing them into a distinctive, memorable melancholia ("Midnight in a Perfect World"'s heartbreaking melange of sampled vocals and guitar melodies) leavened by ecstatic sampling exercises (the self-explanatory "Organ Donor").

Shadow wasn't the only member of Solesides to find his artistic voice outside of the now defunct camp (which continues on as Quannum, an artists' collective that often licenses its works to various record companies of all sizes): Blackalicious aligned themselves with the neo-soul movement, bridging hip-hop with R&B and spoken word (*Nia*,

Blazing Arrow), while Lateef and Lyrics Born, who are still working on their long-awaited solo albums, evolved into a sterling live act.

In contrast, Shadow's *Endtroducing*, released on Mo' Wax and distributed in the United States by A&M Records, inaugurated the concept of the DJ as auteur, a self-contained unit capable of creating albums without the use of outside musicians or, more importantly, an MC. It was a paradigm shift (later confirmed by the underground success of Bomb Records' *Return of the DJ* compilations and Japanese producer DJ Krush's *Milight*), which eclipsed Solesides' dreams of creating a successful label without major label distribution. Still, Solesides' idealism is part and parcel with Shadow's worldview, even though he chooses to express it as a world-weary yet unshaken belief in the redemptive power of hip-hop culture.

by Billy Jam

Too $hort: Born to Mack (Dangerous/Jive, 1988)

Too $hort:
Born to Mack

Since his beginnings twenty years ago as a young teen in East Oakland slanging homemade rap tapes, Too $hort has dropped a shitload of albums and compilations. All are good; some are better than others, but *Born to Mack,* if only for its classics "Freaky Tales" and "Dope Fiend Beat," is a must-have. Released in 1988, it was the first album from the nasty-mouthed but much-loved Oakland rapper on New York's Jive Records after years of selling underground tapes. Eclipsing the music industry's practice of applying "Explicit Lyrics" warning stickers to albums by a few years, Too $hort was already stamping his own warnings: the cover of *Born to Mack* heeds "Dirty Rapps Inside. Parental Guidance Suggested." And that's what *Born to Mack* delivers: dirty raps, freaky tales, and more fiction than fact, all relayed through Too $hort's gifted storytelling coming straight from the streets of "O-A-K-L-A-N-D."

"An M-A-C-K from Oakland, Cal-I-forn-I-A, I'm Too $hort, baby, no I don't play / I'm mackin'," he boldly brags in "Mack Attack." Too $hort, the rap alter ego of the polite and unassuming Todd Shaw, is the ultimate mack persona throughout the album as he takes the listener into his pimp/playboy $hort world, one where a woman is "a tender," a "freak," a "dick pleaser," and, of course, a "beeeyatch" (the word that has consequently become Too $hort's trademark).

"Dope Fiend Beat," which includes the ultimate diss "I know you fine but you look like Lassie, biaaatch," is considered by many to be the "biaaatch anthem," one that is highly revered by such diverse fellow Bay Area artists as E40, DJ Shadow, Mac Dre, and the Invisibl Skratch Piklz, who once built an entire turntable routine around Too $hort's "beeeyatch." Meanwhile, the epic nine-and-a-half-minute "Freaky Tales" is playboy $hort at his pimp/mack daddy, freaky tale-telling best. Sounding young, raw, and full of passion, Too $hort spits his nonstop rhyme tales of female conquests over a booming 808 beat. Notable highlights from the chronicled conquests include: the young tender "Belinda the blender" who "gave head like she made it up" and "was twenty years old with a big round butt"; "Anita … her man's in Santa Rita"; "… Kitty / She was so fine with big fat titties / All night long she was actin' shitty / So I macked on baby like I was Frank Nitti"; and a hooker he meets on Oakland's AC Transit who "… did it for free / On the Foothill bus, number forty-three / All the way in the back she was workin' me / Had my big beat-box and I was jammin' the beat."

The pounding beat with lots of smoldering bass is trademark Too $hort sound. With fat analog 808 beats by Silky C, keyboards by Too $hort, and coproduction by $hort and T. Bohanon, *Born to Mack* is rap music made to be bumped in the trunk. In fact, to make sure fans would indeed be "feeling that bass all down the street," $hort would test out the recordings on his car's system in between studio sessions to see if the bass needed boosting.

$hort also made sure that the DJ was represented. Check DJ Universe's "The Universal Mix," which still sounds fresh fifteen years later. Likewise, "Playboy $hort II," "Little Girls," "Partytime," and "You Know What I Mean," the album's remaining tracks, also sound as good today as they did back in 1988, proving that Too $hort's *Born to Mack* is truly a rap classic, beeeyatch!

2 Live Crew:

by Brett Johnson

As Nasty As They Wanna Be (Luke/Atlantic, 1989)

2 Live Crew:
As Nasty As They
Wanna Be

To 1980s East Coast sophisticates reared on storytelling MCs and funk-spilling breakbeats, Florida's 2 Live Crew may have seemed like pure novelty by the end of the decade. Still, with the Crew's simple, raunchy rhymes and up-tempo, electro-synth soundbeds, they lived up to their name by popularizing the kinetic, booming grooves of Miami bass music. It was dance-rap music served up with call-and-response chants ("Heeeey, we want some pussy!") and booty-shaking beats that thundered, vibrating the concrete. You had to heed 2 Live Crew's command—"Move somethin'"—or get left in Doo Doo Brown's dust.

At the time, rap music was a New York–centric phenomenon save for a wave of gangsta rap that was gaining momentum out West on the coattails of Los Angeles's Ice-T and N.W.A. Plus, hip-hop had yet to really convince mainstream audiences of its musical merit beyond being words chanted over stolen snippets of other songs. In this climate, the Crew was a group of unlikely antiheroes, the redheaded stepchildren of a bastard genre. These four horny dudes from Miami were more concerned about shocking America in a different way—with the explicit details of how many asses they touched rather than the number of caps they could bust. Their vulgar lyrics broke down sexual exploits with women just like their stylistic antecedents —funnymen Blowfly, Dolemite, Richard Pryor, and Redd Foxx—had done a decade earlier.

Largely considered a marginal rap act that made party music for the strip club and fratboy set, frontman Luther "Luke" Campbell, Mr. Mixx, Brother Marquis, and Fresh Kid Ice had released a number of records before their breakthrough album *As Nasty As They Wanna Be* made America blush. And when its lead single "Me So Horny" dropped, the Crew garnered national attention more for the blue content than their music as a moral witch-hunt ensued, led by Tipper Gore's Parents' Music

Resource Center and others. But a diverse group of celebrities—from rocker Bruce Springsteen and folkie Sinead O'Connor to pop star Donny Osmond and even intellectual Henry Louis Gates Jr.—defended Campbell's right to give it to us raw.

Indeed, that's what 2 Live Crew did, mentioning "fuck" 226 times, referring to oral sex 87 times, calling women "bitch" or "ho" some 163 times, and throwing in one nod to incest for good measure. The record is epic in its simultaneous disregard for women as anything other than vessels for sexual pleasure and its wanton pursuit of a good time. The song titles (e.g., "Put Her in the Buck," "Dick Almighty," "The Fuck Shop") do not leave much to the imagination. Says Marquis on "Buck": "It's the way to give her more than she wants / Like the doggystyle, you get all the cunt / 'Cause all men try real hard to do it / … / To have her walkin' funny we try to abuse it / Bitches think a pussy can do it all / So we try real hard just to bust the walls."

At best, the album critiqued sexual stereotypes by its sheer hyperbole with wordplay based in the African-American oral traditions of "dozens," "signifying," and the timeworn practice of exaggerating sexual innuendo. At worst, lines like "Suck my dick, bitch / and make it puke" are jarringly misogynist. Whether Campbell knew at the time that his "facedown, ass-up" rhyme arrangements would make him a First Amendment martyr and an eventual millionaire is debatable. But one thing is certain: The battles fought over *Nasty* made it safe for musicians to speak their minds —no matter how devilishly dirty those minds may be—in the name of artistic freedom.

2Pac:
Me Against the World (Interscope, 1995)
All Eyez on Me (Death Row, 1996)
Makaveli:

by Kris Ex

The Don Killuminati: The 7 Day Theory (Death Row, 1996)

2Pac:
Me Against the World

2Pac:
All Eyez on Me

Makaveli:
The Don Killuminati:
The 7 Day Theory

After all is said and written about Tupac Shakur, there'll still be more to say and write. As of this writing, we're less than two weeks away from the sixth anniversary of his death. And even at this early date, there's no shortage of would-be heirs to the throne of Thug Immortal. But not one of the hopefuls comes close to capturing the magnetism that Pac exuded over men, women, and children from all walks of life. No pretender comes within a Scud's range of the war zone that was Pac's life. With Pac, there's never the need to make things up: the archetypes, patterns, and mythology are there no matter where you turn. Even something as simple as reviewing his best albums presents an interesting arch: the first album was released while he was incarcerated; the second, a mammoth double disc, captured who and what most people think of when they hear Tupac; the final entry, a myth-building posthumous release, created more questions than it answered.

Many Pac fans will gasp in horror when they realize that Pac's first two discs— 1992's *2Pacalypse Now* and 1993's *Strictly 4 My N.I.G.G.A.Z.*—aren't included in this greatest albums list. Just as many will shrug their shoulders, not knowing what the big deal is, as they never heard those records anyway. Pac's first two albums can never be wholly ignored for various reasons. *2Pacalypse Now* was the formative work of an emcee searching for his own voice. Its Black Panther–introduced militancy points to the foundation that tethered all Pac's future endeavors; it's what makes his last album so exciting and so tragic. When he screams "Babylon beware/ I'm coming for the Pharaoh's kids" on *Don Killuminati*'s "Blasphemy," it's the clarion call of a revolutionary come full circle, a ridah returning home on a midnight-black steed with fire in his eyes.

For its part, *Strictly* produced two of Pac's more enduring and emblematic hits, the back-to-back singles that in many ways represented the schism in his life and music. First was "I Get Around," where Pac was only interested in his next sexual conquest, proclaiming with a wide-toothed smile that he "don't stop for hoes." Then, scant months later, he took those same ho's off their knees and placed them on a pedestal with "Keep Ya Head Up." On that song, Pac reminisced how "... Marvin Gaye used to sing to me / He had me feeling like Black was the thing to be." Well, that song will make children of the '90s remember how Tupac had them feeling like Black was the thing to be. As for the album itself, it was uneven at best. And its predecessor was a good record—damned good—but not great.

When Tupac's first truly great album was released, he was behind bars for sexual assault. *Me Against the World* opened with a cinematic lean as newscasts recounted the then current drama in Pac's life: his encounter with a bullet in a '95 shooting at a New York City recording studio and his subsequent exodus from the hospital the next morning, and the dismissal of assault charges from a Halloween '94 confrontation in which he shot two off-duty officers. Produced by a small coterie of trackmasters, the album is slick with in-the-pocket samples from soul icons like Isaac Hayes, Stevie Wonder, and Betty Wright. Even a vocal aside from Redman is transformed into musical beauty.

The themes that would come to define his cannon are in full bloom here: a preoccupation with death ("If I Die 2Nite"), extreme paranoia ("Death Around the Corner"), rebellion without a cause ("Fuck the World"), a Prince Charming syndrome ("Can U Get Away"), and a convoluted Oedipus complex ("Dear Mama"). Throughout, Pac comes across as Michael Corleone in *Godfather III* — he just wants out. On "So Many Tears" he laments, "I'm having visions of leaving here in a hearse / God can you feel me? / Take me away from all the pressure and all the pain / Show me some happiness again / ... / My life is in denial." It must have been a deep denial because on this album, for the first time, Pac sounds confident, secure, and happy to be making music. His delivery is fluid and unforced, an instrument unto itself. He even takes a moment to dedicate "Old School" to hip-hop pioneers, reveling in memories of breakdancing, BVD nylons, tre bags of seeded weed, and a time when "Eric B & Rakim was the shit to me."

On *All Eyez on Me*, Pac takes a swan dive into his outlaw image and comes up drunk with power. Bolstered by the might of Death Row records and overjoyed at being sprung from incarceration, Pac rhymes like he could go on forever over tracks that ride as smooth as a Bentley after a shot of cognac. The album comprises song after song of catharsis. Bitch-baiting abounds, from "Skandalouz" to "Wonda Why They Call U Bitch" to "All About U" to "What'z Ya Phone #," the latter two fueled by samples from Cameo and the Time respectively. Aside from Pac celebrating his rhyming acumen ("Got My Mind Made Up," "No More Pain") and otherwise thumping his chest ("Heartz of Men," "Ambitionz az a Ridah," "Tradin' War Stories," "Can't C Me"), Pac goes sentimental on "Life Goes On" and "I Ain't Mad at Cha," exploring brotherhood, mourning, growth, and loyalty with snapshots of himself, "eyes blurry, saying goodbye at the cemetery." It's with this album that Pac begins to transcend the criteria by which most other rappers are judged. He never emerges as the most gymnastic of wordsmiths, but he comes off as the most honest and the most truthful, the one able to grasp commonalities that cross race, color, and creed. He shows that rage, madness, and the need for vengeance and righteous retribution are not only human, but necessary states of mind. His music becomes experiential, nigh holy. There may not be anything new under this Sun, but that doesn't make it any less hot.

The Don Killuminati: The 7 Day Theory sounds like an album conceived by a man who would fake his own death, as many of Pac's followers claim he has, erroneously believing that Niccolò Machiavelli once simulated his own demise. At the very least it's the music of a man with a death wish. From its opening sequence, which asserts that 2Pac (now known as Makaveli) "is not unavailable for comment," to the vitriolic name-calling first number, "Bomb First," to the initial declaration of war and the sounds of aircraft and machine-gun fire that end "Against All Odds," *The 7 Day Theory* is the anthem of a man who is ready to die or ready to die trying.

Pac's energy spills over the tracks with inkblot messiness, and there's a voyeuristic perversity to be had while getting vicarious thrills from Pac's self-destructive, fatalistic nihilism. When he croons that "Time goes by, puffin' on lye / Hopin' that it gets me high / Got a nigga goin' crazy" with muted, heavy-lidded glee on "Krazy," it's an obvious cry for help; when he equates small artillery with his life partner on "Me and My Girlfriend," he's someone who is so misogynist, he doesn't know whether to distrust women or objectify them and use them; when he talks about his sexpisodes ("I got the bedroom shakin', back-breakin'") on "Toss It Up," he comes off as hurtful and violent. But *Don Killuminati*'s not all fire, brimstone, and bitches. The songs are better constructed than those on *All Eyez on Me*, and in the rare moments when Pac is calm, the result is "To Live & Die in LA," which is as breezy as a Sunday afternoon drop-top ride; "White Man'z World," which is more about uplifting his people than defeating the enemy; and "Just Like Daddy," in which he plays surrogate father to young women, claiming, "Baby, I could take away your pain if you trust me." You're not sure if he can do it, but he believes he can, or at least he wants to so very badly. And what woman could resist that, even as he claims on other lyrics that "[you're] screaming like you're dying every time I'm fucking you"?

And that was Tupac's gift: his ability to lay his soul bare—contradictions, fears, psychosis, and all. What makes these albums classic is not the sound of his beats and rhymes, but the ferocity of his honesty and the thumping of his heart. That his heart has been silenced makes the blood pumping through these discs no less timely or timeless. These albums are hip-hop.

Ultramagnetic MCs:

by Peter Shapiro

Critical Beatdown (Next Plateau, 1988)

Ultramagnetic MCs:
Critical Beatdown

The intro to Ultramagnetic MCs' first demo, "Space Groove" (1984), says pretty much all you need to know about the group that practically invented underground hip-hop: "Space, the final frontier. These are the voyages of the Ultramagnetic MCs: to boldly go where no other rapper has gone before; to examine the universe and reconstruct the style of today's hip-hop culture." Before Kool Keith Thornton, Ced Gee (Cedric Miller), Moe Luv (Maurice Smith), and TR Luv (Trevor Randolph) became hip-hop's first afronauts, they were breakdancers with the New York City Breakers and People's Choice. However, for an individualist like sometime Creedmore and Bellevue resident Kool Keith, breaking didn't allow him to "travel at the speed of thought" and the Bronx residents came together to form one of the greatest rap crews in hip-hop history.

After a thoroughly uncharacteristic first single, "To Give You Love" (1986), Ultramagnetic would begin to make their mark with the mind-boggling "Ego Trippin'" (1986; an edited version is included on *Critical Beatdown*). Featuring epochal production by Ced Gee (with a loop of the drum intro to Melvin Bliss's "Synthetic Substitution," a very occasional synth bassline, and some vicious keyboard stabs, it was the best kind of minimalism, one that managed to fill the entire sound field), "Ego Trippin'" sounded like nothing else at the time, except for maybe Eric B & Rakim's "Eric B Is President" (which is not surprising since Ced Gee helped out on the beats for *Paid in Full* and Boogie Down Productions' *Criminal Minded*, and producer/engineer/cult figure Paul C helped out on *Critical Beatdown*). Adding to the uniqueness factor was Kool Keith, who freestyled utterly deranged rhymes like "As the record just turns / You learn plus burn / By the flame of the lyrics which cooks the human brain, providing overheated knowledge / By means causing pain / Make a migraine…"

"Ego Trippin'"'s blueprint of skeletal sampler schematics and wildly original lyrics was writ large on Ultramagnetic's debut album, *Critical Beatdown*. It may have been a stunning exposition of early sampling technology, but *Critical Beatdown* remains a devastating album in an age of 32-bit samplers and RAM-intensive sound editing software. The music jumps and snaps with an energy reminiscent of the Cold Crush Brothers, while Kool Keith "tak[es] your brain to another dimension" and drops rhymes so abstract (and with cadences so bizarre), they make a Rothko canvas look like a Titian still life.

Ced Gee's production is hyper and choppy—undoubtedly the result of the constraints of his SP-1200 sampler—which makes the music rawer, more immediate, and more febrile, like a raw nerve. Along with Eric B & Rakim's "I Know You Got Soul" and Super Lover Cee & Casanova Rud's "Do the James," *Critical Beatdown* was responsible for rehabilitating the Godfather of Soul. James Brown's clipped guitar lines and grunts are all over this record, and it was Ced Gee's mining of Brown's unique lode of abrasion and funk that made *Critical Beatdown* so original. In fact, the Bomb Squad have often said that *Critical Beatdown* was a major influence on Public Enemy's *It Takes a Nation of Millions to Hold Us Back* (check out the teakettle horn on "Ease Back" for proof).

For all of Ced Gee's creativity and influence, though, it would be Kool Keith that would emerge from the album as the star. Smelling "a grape in the duck preserves," "hang[ing] with Barney Rubble in Bedrock," looking at "your balls of clay with X-vision," Keith would invent underground hip-hop in one fell swoop. Rammellzee was perhaps the only other MC to explore such surreal terrain. But while Rammellzee was trying to remake rap as the most complex graffiti burner, Kool Keith was maintaining a connection with hip-hop's battle rhyme tradition—it's just that he seemed to be imagining a battle between Richard Pryor, Larry Flynt, and Jonathan Winters.

by Jeff Chang

V/A: Wildstyle Original Soundtrack (Animal, 1983; Rhino, 1997)

V/A:
Wildstyle Original
Soundtrack

The meeting took place in Times Square. It was 1980, before NASDAQ or MTV. Instead, it was a carnival of red-bulb burlesque and all-day kung-fu flicks, Five Percent ciphers kicking math, junkies in the alleys with baseball bats.

The summit was held in an abandoned building, a former massage parlor commandeered for art's sake. It was a small meeting between a subversive white East Village filmmaker, a natty do-or-die Bed-Stuy artist, and a Lower East Side *boricua* graf legend, who were creating amidst destruction. Soon Fab 5 Freddy and Charlie Ahearn found themselves in a far corner of the north Bronx, at a party presided over by Chief Rocker Busy Bee (the party-starter who, legend has it, coined the term "hip-hop"), on ground ruled by DJ Breakout, amongst kings and queens without castles or crowns.

Of course, *Wildstyle* was amateurish, but that was hip-hop then—wide-eyed, wide open for anyone who wanted to go there. With genius and desperation, Charlie and Fab conspired to place Lee Quiñones—a reticent, midnight wallcrawler with a talent for pulling beauty and shape from chaos—at the center of the film. Then, all around them, like a force of nature, swirled colors, images, bodies, beats, and words. "Get the point?" the hurricane sang. "*We're* the joint."

In 1982, when hip-hop rolled across the world like a tsunami, the *Wildstyle* movie, soundtrack, and world tour answered the question *What is "hip-hop"?* Early reviewers treated the entire experience as a tourist trip to the rough side of town, an artless curiosity presenting the low risk of three-card monte game. (Busy Bee and Lil' Rodney Cee rapping about grabbing headlines in the *Daily* and the *Post* must have seemed as quaint to them as it seems ironic to us now after decades of media rap rage.) But *Wildstyle* now endures as much more than art; it is a true school parchment, a hip-hop class requirement, "the four elements" frozen in amber.

At the time, the project was blessed by luck and secured by the producers' boundless curiosity and improvisational genius. During Charlie and Fab's year-long advanced seminar in the post-"Rapper's Delight" club scene, they walked into a marquee rivalry between Charlie Chase's Cold Crush Brothers and Grand Wizard Theodore's Fantastic Freaks. They added wickedly exciting dubplate special riddims —cut by Blondie's Chris Stein with Fab and a downtown white-boy crew, and recut Bronx-style by Theodore, Chase, DST, and KK Rockwell—then captured three of the most electrifying, influential ensemble routines ever committed to tape.

Here's Fantastic's Prince Whipper Whip— "I am the New Yorker, the sweet walker, the woman stalker, the jive talker, the money maker"—bragging about being "the least conceited." And he is undefeated, at least until Cold Crush's JDL dispenses him with a shrug: "If you still got money and you wanna bet, well I bet a hundred dollars that I'm not whipped yet." Caught on the stoop and in the limo, at the Dixie and the Amphitheater, the words rock and tumble into all kinds of intriguing vectors: Schoolly D's "Saturday Night," LL Cool J's "Dear Yvette," Smoothe Da Hustler's "Broken Language." They're the engravings on a rap Rosetta Stone.

But to emphasize the soundtrack's historical weight is to miss the point. *Wildstyle* still feels like *now*. Charlie and Fab never tried to cork the ferocious competitive energy, the feverish call-and-response, the phantasmic sense of possibility present in a hip-hop moment. On the contrary, *Wildstyle* remains the only hip-hop film and soundtrack that adequately conveys the communal thrill of merging with the tide, riding the lightning.

If the moment of *Wildstyle* must be fixed, it is the night before Reagan's morning, sad mourning, in America. Shockdell is talking homelessness like a prophet. Ikonoklast panzer Rammellzee strides onstage waving a sawed-off shotgun in one hand, reaching down and pulling rhymes out of his pocket with the other. One second he's stepping out at Cypress Hills, beating down a toy with his def graffiti, the next he's signing off with an apple-pie flourish, shouting out the Rock Steady on the linoleum and the cops in the crowd. That ricochet unpredictability, that badder-than-bold, bolder-than-bad chest-thumping, the volatile combo of sociology-shattering disbelief and Sunday-morning faith it inspired in anyone it touched—all this is *Wildstyle*'s gift.

Wu-Tang Clan:
Enter The Wu-Tang (36 Chambers) (Loud, 1993)
Raekwon: Only Built 4 Cuban Linx... (Loud, 1995)
Ghostface Killah: Ironman (Razor Sharp/Epic, 1996)

by Jon Caramanica

Wu-Tang Clan:
Enter The Wu-Tang
(36 Chambers)

Raekwon:
Only Built 4 Cuban Linx...

Ghostface Killah:
Ironman

Eight MCs. Kung-fu iconography. Multiple aliases. Masks. Crisp and nasty snares. Swords. Shaolin. Semifluid membership. Solo successes. Manicures. Mafia fetish. Chess. Triumph. Hoodies. Hoax split-ups. Prison. Bullet train. Jesus. Killa bees. Humility. Perpetual imbroglios. Polo goose. Exhumed soul music, vigorously inhaling new life. Ice cream. Welfare. Black pride. Darts. Chicken-and-broccoli wallabees. Monks. The muthafuckin' ruckus. Empire.

Unlikely. It's the only word to truly capture the ascendance of the Wu-Tang Clan, who from the moment they first emerged from some mythologized urban underground in 1992 not only made a significant impact on hip-hop music, but also permanently rearranged the genre's business practices. Before Wu, extended crews were a liability. Before Wu, the notion of rappers entering businesses other than rapping was laughable. Before Wu, releasing a 12-inch single independently seemed like a quaint idea. Before Wu, pop-rap seemed like a cruel inevitability.

But with one simple song, 1992's "Protect Ya Neck," the rules got changed. Released on the Clan's own "label," Wu-Tang Records, it attracted considerable industry attention and got unusual underground radio support. Soon, the Wu were scooped up by upstart label Loud Records, which was helping to relocate New York as the center of street-influenced rap after years of falling behind Los Angeles in the race for the territorial throne. Wu-Tang would prove central to that mission.

The group's debut album, *Enter The Wu-Tang (36 Chambers)*, posited new guidelines for the genre. No longer was it sufficient merely to unleash a series of morbid poses to qualify as gangster. Wu-Tang took a far more psychological route through the pain and its causes rather than only worrying (and rhyming) about its consequences. The Wu hailed from Staten Island, the only New York borough that had not yet made a firm footprint on the city's hip-hop scene. With their debut, they made it sound every bit as foreboding as the locales they were seeking to overtake.

And chaotic, too. In large part, "Protect Ya Neck" worked because of its furious, anarchic arrangement. Some MCs got sixteen bars, some got four. The hook arrived at odd intervals. Producer and Clan "abbot" RZA created an aesthetic of barely controlled radioactive spill, augmenting the standard drum arrangements with jabbing horns, horror-movie squeals, and the odd kung-fu insertion. Each Clan member got a turn, and the song closed out with GZA's vicious skewering of the industry they were about to overtake: "First of all, who's your A&R? / A mountain climber who plays an electric guitar? / But he don't know the meaning of dope / when he's lookin' for a suit-and-tie rap that's cleaner than a bar of soap / And I'm the dirtiest thing in sight / Matter of fact, bring out the girls and let's have a mud fight."

Said mud fight sprawled over a dozen tracks, loosely connected by skits and sampled ideologies from the Clan's favorite martial arts warriors. "Can It Be All So Simple" was perhaps hip-hop's first wistful song, a textured remembrance of times that weren't necessarily better—an addict father, devastating violence, wakes. The truth was, it never was so simple, as proved by "C.R.E.A.M." (Cash Rules Everything Around Me), the perfect companion song to "Simple." On this deeply grim record of the pathologies of the small-time criminal with an eye on bigger and deader, Raekwon maps out the blueprint: "Running up in gates and doing hits for high stakes / ... / my life got no better, same damn 'Lo sweater / ... / Figured out I went the wrong routes / So I got with a sick-ass clique and went all out / ... / ... every week we made forty Gs."

The air of tragic inevitability hung heavy over *Enter the Wu-Tang*, thanks largely to the production of RZA. A sonic homogenizer of profound skill, he almost single-handedly created the imagined world that the Wu represented. Whether he was sampling a classical string section, a grizzly blues singer, or up-tempo, get-in-on-the-good-foot funk, he manipulated it to his own ends, creating a Spector-like wall of sound—brassy, dirty, rugged—that the rest of the Clan had to rap through, instead of on top of.

It's something of a miracle, then, that the members managed to develop personalities as distinct as they did. Sex symbol Method Man, who had an eponymous song on the Wu debut that proved to be its biggest, was the first Wu member to go solo, releasing *Tical* in 1994 on the powerhouse hip-hop label Def Jam. But despite his palatability—or, more frankly, because of it—he never truly captured the Wu ethos.

That task fell on the Clan's two most compellingly sinister minds: Raekwon and Ghostface Killah. Ol' Dirty Bastard had the unhinged schizoid personality, and both GZA/Genius and Inspectah Deck had meticulous, perfectionist flows. But Rae and Ghost—incredibly close friends—had a gift for bringing a stunningly high level of analysis to situations that most rappers might recount without thinking twice: relationships, drug deals, childhood gone wild. For most artists, these were mere details to flesh out boasts. For Rae and Ghost, they were the very lifeblood of their art.

Raekwon's debut, *Only Built 4 Cuban Linx …*, was the first Wu project to pick up where *Enter the Wu-Tang* had left off. Drenched again in RZA sonics, it remains the most thoroughly realized among Wu albums, anchored by Raekwon, who was the first Clan member to fully comprehend hip-hop's reliance on character and narrative. On "Knowledge God," which announces the gravity of its subject matter with orchestral bombast and sneaky piano trills, Raekwon proves his gift for thick description, describing a soon-to-be-overtaken foe thusly: "Mafia flicks / tyin' up tricks was his main hobby / Teachin' his seed Wu-Tang karate / Mixin' drinks in clubs / Hairy chest with many minks / Nighttime rollin' with spics / Extra live, he claimed he couldn't die / Top ranked, sixteen shots in his fishtank."

"Rainy Dayz" was a loose update of the excellent "Tearz" from the Wu's debut. Again, sampled strings juxtapose with a slightly awkward but full-bodied female R&B vocal to approximate the cover of darkness. "Verbal Intercourse" is so foreboding a song, it makes even guest MC Nas, no avatar of thuggishness, sound dark and nihilistic. And "Incarcerated Scarfaces" is among the most iconic Wu performances ever. RZA's beat is positively propulsive, heavy on cymbal and bass, constantly interrupted by the sound of a train disappearing in the distance. Accordingly, Rae delivers a breathless performance of seeming non sequiturs that miraculously jell into a coherent fire, thanks to complex internal rhyme schemes and the ever-present snarl of a man who's seen it all and has no choice but to tell his tales.

Ghostface Killah's first album, *Ironman*, arrived a year after *Cuban Linx*, although the tenor he was seeking to strike was clear from his harried monologue on the intro to Rae's debut: "You know how my heart feels … I got shot at, man, my mom's windows got shot the fuck up, man. My baby's in here, god. I got to take time and raise my family, man." Ghost isn't one to idly boast or brag, and while his debut certainly had its share of self-promotion, it also introduced the concept of the thug as fragile emotional being. Indeed, *Ironman* is almost completely about pathos. Later on, Ghost would dub his sound the "crying style," and that's exactly what it is: a high-pitched screech that uses the upper register as a palette of angst.

"Motherless Child" flips a pair of blues samples into a moving template for hood remembrance. On "All That I Got Is You," Mary J. Blige guests on a transcendent paean to Ghost's mother, a woman who triumphed through struggle: "… my whole youth was sharper than cleats / … / But I remember this, moms would lick her fingertips / To wipe the cold out my eye before school with her spit." And "Wildflower" remains the most tortured assessment of volatile love ever expressed in hip-hop— and perhaps in pop. It's easy to read it as misogynist, but it's more honest to understand it as the sometimes misguided rantings of a man driven beyond the edge by infidelity. Out of all the rappers in the genre, only Ghost could toe that line and not lose.

Pain aside, *Ironman* doesn't lack for sheer flame-throwing energy. The posse cut "Winter Warz" is one of the Wu's finest moments. Ghost partners with Raekwon and Cappadonna on "Daytona 500," which samples the sound of a car whipping around a racetrack turn and pairs it with an irrepressibly funky bassline (best Ghost line: "I slapbox with Jesus, and lick shots at Joseph"). And on that single's B-side, "Camay," a delicate piano tinkle and an earnest crooning male vocal underlie an utterly lascivious ode to the fairer sex. But even here, Ghost and his brethren aren't overly lecherous. The best features of their objects of affection: assistant manager at Paragon Sports, killer baked macaroni and turkey wings, eyeglasses, quiet and shy, loves kids.

Notes on Contributors

Editor

Oliver Wang, who occasions out in public as O-Dub, lives and works out of Oakland, California. Since 1994 he has been actively writing on music, culture, and race for the *San Francisco Bay Guardian*, *LA Weekly*, *Minneapolis City Pages*, *URB*, *The Source*, *Vibe*, AsianAvenue.com, Popmatters.com, and other regional and national publications. He also is working on a PhD dissertation at UC Berkeley, focusing on the Bay Area's Pilipino-American disc jockey community. In his increasingly rare spare time, Oliver is an active radio/club DJ, avid record collector, and amateur photographer. In an alternate timeline, he might have been vying to become the first Asian-American Supreme Court Justice, but he's pretty happy with his current reality. For more information, visit www.o-dub.com.

Foreword Writer

Dante Ross. Born on November 10, 1967, this San Francisco– born, New York–raised pizza bagel (i.e., Italian-Jew) was reared in Manhattan's Lower East Side on a steady diet of Led Zeppelin, Sarcasm, Old Skool hip-hop, and rice and beans. Among other things, Mr. Ross, along with partner John Gamble, is one half of the Grammy Award–winning production team (Carlos Santana, *Supernatural*), the Stimulated Dummies. He served as executive producer on *One for All* (Brand Nubian) and *Mecca and the Soul Brother* (Pete Rock & CL Smooth), and produced Grand Puba, 3rd Bass, Del the Funkee Homosapien, and Everlast (the triple-platinum *Whitey Ford Sings the Blues*). In his spare time, Mr. Ross likes to go beat digging, watch Old Skool skateboard videos, and listen to Stevie Wonder with his dog Sunny while watching *Flip Wilson* reruns.

Senior Contributors

Elizabeth Mendez Berry was raised in Toronto, Canada. While studying Political Science and Literature at the University of Toronto, she walked into the local alternative weekly, *eye*, and pitched a story on El Vez, the Mexican Elvis. It was rejected, but the editor let her choose the CDs she was interested in reviewing. She walked out with M.O.P., MC Lyte, and a new hustle. Since then she's written about music, poetry, and politics for publications including *Blu*, *Bust*, the *Globe and Mail*, and *URB*. She currently resides in Brooklyn, works in Manhattan at *Vibe* magazine, and *parrandeas* in Jackson Heights, Queens, where she's a member of the Movement for Peace in Colombia and where they have the best *arepas de choclo* outside of Antioquia.

Jon Caramanica contributes regularly to *Rolling Stone*, *XXL*, *The Source*, *Spin*, *Vibe*, the *Village Voice*, and *Vice*. A former editor of *Trace* and an on-sabbatical doctoral candidate in sociology, he is currently at work on his first book.

Jeff Chang was born of Chinese and Native Hawaiian ancestry in the dimming spring before the long, hot summer almost eight years after statehood. At an early age, his father taught him it was American to side with the underdog. He still believes in the latter. The author of *Can't Stop, Won't Stop: A History of the Hip-Hop Generation*, he was formerly the Senior Editor of Politics at Russell Simmons' 360hiphop.com, a founding editor of *ColorLines* magazine, and a cofounder of Solesides. He lives with his wife, Lourdes, and two sons, Jonathan and Solomon, in Berkeley, California, a state of mind halfway between Brooklyn and Hawaii.

Tony Green is a seventh grade language arts teacher and National Arts Journalism Program Fellow who, when he isn't hanging out with his wife, Dena, plays guitar in the Tampa Bay–based jazz-funk band Jes' Grew, watches *Courage the Cowardly Dog*, and hosts the *Grooves* show on Tampa's WMNF 88.5 FM. He has written about hip-hop, soul, rock, funk, and jazz for *The Source, Vibe, Spin, XXL*, the *Village Voice*, and numerous other major outlets.

Hua Hsu writes about culture and politics for the *Village Voice, VIBE, The Wire*, the *San Francisco Bay Guardian, URB, Blender, ColorLines*, and several other publications. He currently lives in Cambridge, Massachussetts, where he has grown to accept that "there's always next year" for the Red Sox. He is currently a PhD candidate in the History of American Civilization program at Harvard University. He hopes to complete his dissertation on American democracy and the Transpacific imagination sometime this century.

Joseph Patel is a writer living in New York City. Under his own name and his superhero alter ego Jazzbo, he has scribed for a number of publications through the years, covering music and greater pop culture, including everything from glitch-hop rap superstars to nubile young supermodels (his favorite). Patel's work has been found in *Vice, Mass Appeal, URB, Flaunt, The Source, Vibe, XXL, Dazed & Confused*, the *Village Voice, The Face*, and others. Often cast as a "hater," Patel maintains he is "hated," a misunderstood romantic whose cynicism is born of unfulfilled idealism. Patel wishes he were as adroit as James Tai.

Peter Shapiro is one of the world's leading authorities on air guitar and a journalist whose work has appeared in *The Wire, Spin, The Independent, URB, Time Out,* and *Sleaze Nation.*

Dave Tompkins has written for *Village Voice, The Wire, ego trip,* and *The Bomb.* The first double-dutch rhymes he heard came from Boris Karloff reading "Jumping Joan." Dave's book, *Reason For a Very Spliced Day,* will come out because the public is dying to know about The Awesome Of Course Crew. His forthcoming illustrated electro book, *I Have No Vocoder and I Must Scream,* is coming out with a hand from the good folks at the Broken Wrist Project.

Contributors

Alistair "Lefty" Banks, bedroom critic/cynic extraordinaire, honed his craft through years of email-flaming and newsgroup-battling. An erstwhile contributor to *URB* magazine, Swedish design catalogs, and his former 'zine, *In Search of DJ EZ-Rock,* he's currently working on his first book, a memoir entitled *Fake Friends and Industry Whores: How I Made My Living Off Hip-Hop.* Currently roaming nomadically out West, he's on the run from the righteous fury of the Folks Beneath the Escalator.

Reginald Dennis. A former Music Editor at *The Source* and the creator and founder of *XXL* magazine, Reggie spends most of his leisure time chilling hard, living in luxury, and giving out far too much free advice.

Kris Ex writes for people. In the past, he's edited for people. But now, he just writes for people that edit.

Allen Gordon is a surly old cuss who is at the end of his wits and has a strange fascination with Bruce Wayne, turkey sandwiches with no mayo, and the color blue. When he's not lifting weights or reading comic books, you can find him wandering the streets conversing with himself, saying, "Fuck that, I throw harder than Greg Maddux! Just one more slice, mom, please!" Gordon is currently undergoing psychiatric evaluation at Arkham Asylum.

Ernest Hardy was born in Birmingham, Alabama, just as shit was hitting the fan (i.e., fire hoses, police dogs, marches, and sit-ins.) He attended Cass Technical High School in Detroit and then UCLA in … LA … where he majored in English Lit. He currently resides in Hollywood, California, where he's working on a book of poetry (titled *Crackhead Ramblings & Pickaninny Poses*) and compiling a collection of his criticism. He's also a cofounder of the new New Negro arts collective BAM! Sistafuckah. His work has appeared in *Rolling Stone*, the *LA Times*, the *New York Times*, and *LA Weekly*. He doesn't actually read these publications. He is a Sundance Fellow.

Todd Inoue is Music Editor at the *San José Metro* and Contributing Editor at *Tower Pulse* magazine. His work has appeared in *Vibe, URB, Transworld, Giant Robot*, and many now-defunct websites. He lives in San José with his wife, Betty. He plays soccer, eats natto, and putters around the house.

With an emphasis on Bay Area hip-hop, **Billy Jam** has been a music journalist since 1987 and was among the original hip-hop reporters for *The Source* magazine. He has also written for numerous other publications, including *Vibe, Murder Dog, XXL, BOMB Hip Hop*, and the *San Francisco Bay Guardian*. He won the 1997 Music Journalism Award for an investigative feature for the *San Francisco Chronicle* newspaper on incarcerated rapper Rappin' 4-Tay. Jam has also contributed to a number of books, including the *Vibe History of Hip Hop* and Vibe's book on Tupac. He recently finished a book on world champion scratch DJ Q-Bert. Additionally, Jam heads the mixed media company Hip Hop Slam (www.hiphopslam.com).

Brett Johnson is the Senior Editor at *The Source*, a magazine about hip-hop music, culture, and politics. The former reporter for the *LA Times* and the *Hartford Courant* has written for a number of magazines, including *Essence, Savoy*, and *Vibe*, where he also held the Senior Editor position. Johnson has also written for MTV's *Chart Attack*, a weekly music news program. Currently, the Cal-Berkeley and NYU graduate lives in Brooklyn, New York.

Serena Kim, twenty-nine, lives in Brooklyn, New York, with her husband, Jeff. By day she is the diligent Senior Editor in *Vibe* magazine's music department (she's also contributed to *The Source, The Fader, XXL*, and *Split: Stories from a Generation Raised on Divorce*). By night she is a pot-smoking couch potato who plays vintage arcade games and watches skate videos, which is no small wonder since she grew up in LA and attended UCSC. She misses California because her favorite thing is how music sounds in an apartment with hardwood floors on a warm, lemony yellow afternoon. She hopes to someday write a book.

Melissa Maerz is the Music Editor at *City Pages* in Minneapolis, as well as the former and future drummer for the currently defunct experimental band F-matic. Her articles have appeared in *Spin, The Rocket,* and *Badaboom Gramophone* amongst others, and they have been used for everything from required reading in a class that Greil Marcus teaches at Princeton to newsprint fish wrap. Check out www.city-pages.com for examples of her writing.

NYC-based scribe (and part-time DJ) **Chairman (Jefferson) Mao** has written for a buncha music publications, but, honestly, none of 'em were worth diddly-squat compared with *ego trip,* the 'zine he and his cronies slaved over for thirteen issues before pulling the plug in 1998. In 1999, he coauthored the acclaimed hip-hop fac-toid-filled tome, *ego trip's Book of Rap Lists* and executive-produced its supa-superb accompanying soundtrack, *ego trip's The Big Playback.* Fall 2002 saw Mao et amigos drop *ego trip's Big Book of Racism!* on an unsuspecting public. Buy it and give the gift of hate this holiday season.

Mosi Reeves is a freelance journalist based in Oakland, California. An Editor-at-Large for *Kitchen Sink* magazine, he frequently contributes articles on music and culture to the *San Francisco Bay Guardian,* the *San José Mercury News, URB, The Wire UK, SOMA,* and several other publications. He is currently working on a book about hip-hop music.

Chris Ryan was born and raised in Philadelphia. He now lives in Brooklyn where has a dog, a broken turntable, and a fake gold chain with a 76ers emblem on it. His writing has sporadically appeared in *Spin,* the *Village Voice,* and *Hit It or Quit It.*

Joe Schloss's book, *Making Beats: The World of Sample-Based Hip-Hop*, will be published by Wesleyan University Press as part of its Music/Culture series. He holds a PhD in ethnomusicology and lives in Brooklyn, New York, where he enjoys digging for beats, eating knishes, and arguing with people.

Zenobia Simmons is a self-described hardworking hip-hop High Priestess who specializes in music journalism and tarot cards. She also occasionally dabbles in PR and radio. One of her greatest accomplishments is creating, writing, compiling, and editing liner notes for the three-volume all-female rap compilation *Fat Beats & Bra Straps* on Rhino Records. Zenobia is currently holding it down in Brick City, Florida, trying to make the world safe for her unborn babies and battling the forces of wackness.

David Toop is a composer, author, critic, and sound curator. He has published three books: *Rap Attack* (first published in 1984, now in its third edition), *Ocean of Sound*, and *Exotica* (a winner of the Before Columbus Foundation American Book Award 2000). He has written for many publications, including *The Wire*, *The Face*, *The Times*, the *New York Times, URB*, and *Bookforum*. In 2000, he curated Sonic Boom for the Hayward Gallery in London, the UK's biggest exhibition of sound art. His first album was released on Brian Eno's Obscure label in 1975, and since 1995 he has released six solo CDs. See www.david-toop.com.